Feeding the Under 5s

Allan Dyson and Lucy Meredith

 David Fulton Publishers

The authors would like to thank the staff and children at Oak Tree Day Nursery and Charlton Nursery, Karen Jarvis at First Steps Centre for Children and Families, and Rachel Ladd.

This edition reprinted 2007 by Routledge
2 Park Square, Milton Park, Abingdon, Oxon, OX14 4RN
Simultaneously published in the USA and Canada
By Routledge
270 Madison Avenue, New York, NY 10016

First published in Great Britain in 2006 by David Fulton Publishers

10 9 8 7 6 5 4 3 2

British Library Cataloguing in Publication Data
A catalogue record for this book is available from the British Library.

ISBN-10: 1 84312 388 6
EAN: 978 184312 388 0

Typeset by FiSH Books, Enfield, Middlesex
Printed and bound in Great Britain

Feeding the
Under 5s

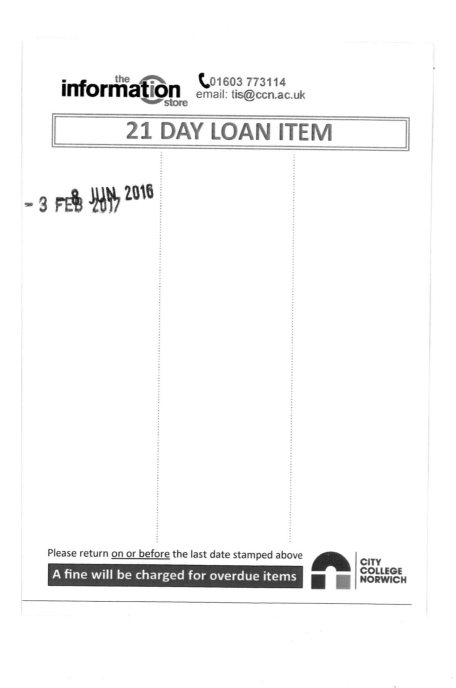

the **information** store

☎ 01603 773114
email: tis@ccn.ac.uk

21 DAY LOAN ITEM

- 3 FEB 2017
8 JUN 2016

Please return <u>on or before</u> the last date stamped above

A fine will be charged for overdue items

CITY
COLLEGE
NORWICH

Contents

Introduction

This book is about improving children's diets. Its focus is on the importance of diet in the growth and development of children, and the prevention of food-related diseases in childhood and later life. It provides both the underlying theory to explain dietary and food safety guidelines, and practical advice and information on sensible, achievable and safe ways of improving children's diet.

Children's diets are made up from anything that they eat and drink. From a biological perspective, food provides children with nutrients that they need to carry out normal daily activities. A healthy diet is about eating a variety of foods to get the right balance of nutrients. The first two chapters cover the key issues concerning food and nutrition, and its importance in feeding under fives a healthy diet. It is a truism that there are no bad foods, only bad diets. Unless a child has a particular allergy or intolerance, there are few foods that she or he should not eat. In theory, it is not difficult to provide a healthy diet for young children but current research suggests that many children's diets are becoming unhealthier. Why?

Most babies up to about six months normally consume only breast or formula milk and, below the age of two, children are almost wholly dependent on adults. As children develop and become more independent they have more influence on what they eat, but under fives diets are still largely dependent on the food provided by parents and carers. Adults have a significant influence on the quality children's diets, and eating patterns developed in childhood continue to impact on food choices throughout adolescence and adulthood. Our food choices depend on a variety of conscious and unconscious decisions, which are influenced by social, cultural, psychological and economic factors. Even though we may be aware of the principles of healthy eating these other factors are often dominant. Children usually eat the same types of food as the rest of the family and adult eating habits, good or bad, are likely to be copied and perpetuated by children. To improve children's diets it may be necessary for parents and carers to modify their own food choices. Chapter 3 considers some of the issues surrounding food choice.

There are clear links between diet and health. Under fives grow and develop more rapidly than at any other time in their lives and a correct balance of nutrients is vital. Many nutrients, particularly vitamins and minerals, have specific functions. Too little, or sometimes too much, can adversely effect children's health and normal development. A poor diet may not result in clear or obvious symptoms – it may be that a child is simply more tired or irritable than usual. However, some deficiencies can cause more serious, longer term problems such as impaired physical or mental development. An increasing problem in children of all ages is eating too much food, particularly those foods which are high in fat and sugar. Obesity is reaching epidemic proportions in children. Since the mid-1980s, childhood obesity has almost doubled and some estimates suggest that 50 per cent of children will be overweight by 2020. Obesity can cause psychological as well as physical problems in childhood and later in life. There are links between obesity, diabetes, heart disease and some types of cancer. Overweight or obese children are more likely to have the same characteristics in adulthood. Chapter 4 investigates the links between diet and health.

A balanced diet provides all the nutrients children need to maintain their health and wellbeing. Childhood diets often determine eating patterns later in life; developing healthy eating habits at a young age can protect against diseases in both the long and short term. There is increasing evidence that there is an imbalance between children's diets – what they actually eat – and their nutritional needs. Although we may understand what a healthy balanced diet is, and try to get children to eat healthily, we face the problem of turning theory into practice. This is particularly challenging in the childcare settings. It is expected that the food that is provided while children are in day care should be nutritious and healthy. Providing a balanced diet is one thing, but persuading children to eat it is quite another. This is a particular problem where children have been used to eating inappropriate foods at home. Research shows that nutrition education is best achieved by embedding food and health as part of the curriculum or range of activities that are available to children, and that any other difficulties surrounding food and feeding are best dealt with as part of the behaviour management policy of the nursery or childcare setting. Chapter 5 discusses the issues which need to be considered when developing feeding strategies and uses four case studies to examine their policy and practice.

Last but not least, food needs to be safe to eat. With increasing attention given to the nutritional content of foods, it is easy to lose sight of food hygiene issues. It is a requirement in the UK that food should be manufactured and prepared hygienically. All businesses that prepare or serve food must register with the local authority and comply with relevant food hygiene regulations. Chapter 6 introduces the basic principles of food hygiene and suggests practical measures that could be taken to ensure food is produced in a safe and hygienic way.

CHAPTER 1

Healthy eating and the under 5s

- What are children made of...?
- Summary of healthy eating principles
- Vegetarian diets
- Vitamin supplements
- Dental hygiene
- Foods to eat in moderation

Introduction

Food provides the nutrients necessary to sustain normal growth and development in the early years. The weight of babies has normally tripled by the time of their first birthday and their height will have almost doubled. This rate of development slows in the second year of life but remains comparatively rapid. From the age of about two, height increases about 6 cm annually through childhood and adolescence. In the first five years of life a child's brain will have grown to about 90 per cent of its final size. Associated with height and weight is the development of hair and teeth and, unseen, internal organs such as the heart and lungs. Normal growth and development are dependent on many factors, one of the most important being the quality of diet.

At birth, a baby's diet is totally dependent on breast or formula milk. Most experts recommend breast milk because it contains all the nutrients needed in the correct proportions. In addition, evidence suggests that breastfeeding reduces the risk of infection and diseases, in both the short and long term. The Department of Health recommends that exclusive breastfeeding should continue until six months when weaning – the gradual introduction of solid food into the diet – can begin. At six months, breast milk may not be providing all the nutrients that a baby needs and the introduction of other foods enables the provision of a balanced diet. In particular, babies may become deficient in iron and the introduction of puréed meat or pulses is a good idea. Weaning should not normally begin before a baby reaches 20 weeks.

If weaning does start before six months, there are a number of foods that should be avoided, particularly those than contain: wheat, gluten (a protein found in wheat), eggs, fish, shellfish, liver, citrus fruits, nuts, soft and unpasteurised cheeses.

Weaning enables nutrients from a greater variety of foods to be eaten and develops other skills in infants such as biting and chewing. When children are first weaned the solid food should be smooth and puréed, gradually changing to a thicker consistency with some 'lumps'. By the time children are about one year old food will be the same as for the rest of the family but mashed and chopped into small manageable pieces. Once weaning has started children are no longer dependent only on breast milk and provision of a healthy balanced diet starts to take on importance. It is essential, therefore, that family food provides a healthy diet for the benefit of young and old alike.

A healthy balanced diet provides all the nutrients that children need, in the correct amounts. These days, general concerns about children's diets are twofold. The first is that children are eating too much food – more than they need to meet their energy requirements. When this happens the excess is converted into body fat which increases the risk of becoming overweight or obese. The second concern is that there are insufficient nutrients in children's diets to maintain normal growth and to undertake their daily activities. It is quite possible for a child to eat too much food and become overweight whilst, at the same time, be undernourished because her or his diet lacks sufficient of the essential nutrients. The effects of a poor childhood diet may only become apparent in later life.

Children should enjoy food; it is one of the pleasures of life. It is best to avoid thinking about 'good' or 'bad' foods – the key point is that children should eat a healthy balanced diet. This chapter discusses some of the core issues that relate to eating a healthy diet. It starts by looking at the principles on which a healthy diet is based and considering how these may be applied to young children. There are a number of foods that, if eaten to excess, can lead to long or short term health problems and guidance is given on some foods that should be avoided or limited.

What are children made of...?

Children's bodies are made up of *cells*. No one really knows how many cells they have – it increases as they grow and by the time they reach adulthood it is likely to be in the order of 10 to 100 trillion (a trillion is a million million or 1,000,000,000,000). Children (like adults) have *tissues* – groups of cells with similar structure and function – muscle or nervous tissues are examples, which increase in size and number as they grow. *Organs* comprise two or more types of tissue that together perform a particular function – the heart and brain are examples of organs. Finally, *organ systems* are a group of organs working together to achieve a particular function. For example the heart, blood and blood vessels combine to form the circulatory system. They work together to transport nutrients and oxygen throughout the body and remove waste products. Figures 1.1 and 1.2 illustrate the typical composition of a child's body.

Cells consist mainly of water but they contain also many substances that are essential for life. The food that children eat provides nutrients for cells, which are essential for normal metabolism. The nutrients are needed for energy and for growth – the development of new cells – that enable the enlargement of tissues and organs. Cells are constantly changing – new substances are being produced

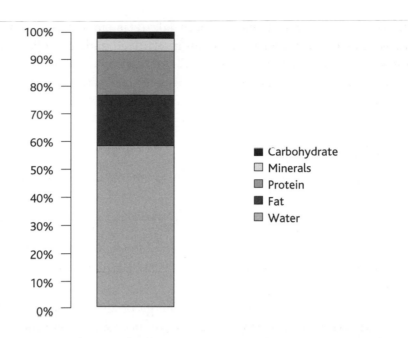

The largest constituent of a child's body is water – nearly two-thirds. The amount of fat is highly variable between individuals as well as variations due to age and gender. Most of the minerals are found in bones and teeth although iron is an important constituent of blood. Many minerals are present in cells in minute quantities but play a vital role in metabolism. Carbohydrates are present mainly as blood sugar and as glycogen which is stored in the liver. Although essential, vitamins only occur in very small amounts – too small to register on this chart.

Figure 1.1 Approximate composition of a child's body

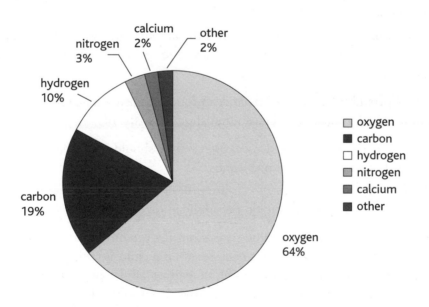

Oxygen is the most abundant element found. It is a constituent of water (H_2O), fats, proteins and carbohydrates. Carbon and hydrogen are major constituents of fats, proteins and carbohydrates. Nitrogen is found in protein (and other important substances such as DNA and RNA). Calcium is present in significant quantities in bones and teeth. 'Other' includes minerals such as phosphorous, sodium, potassium and iron plus various trace elements.

Figure 1.2 Approximate percentages of elements in a child's body

and waste material is being excreted. It is amazingly complex – there are thousands of chemical reactions, all interlinked and controlled by enzymes, going on all the time. A healthy balanced diet ensures that the cells receive the nutrients they need to enable a child's body to function effectively, and maintain health and wellbeing.

Healthy eating

Food is defined as any solid or liquid that contains nutrients. Children need nutrients for:

- Energy – normal, active children depend on food to provide sufficient energy.
- Growth and repair – children need food to enable normal growth and development, and to repair and replace tissues that wear out or become damaged.
- Regulating their body functions – energy production and growth are not random events and children have substances such as enzymes and hormones to control the activities of their bodies.

Healthy eating guidelines for under 5s are similar to those recommended for adults but there are some differences. When planning meals and snacks for under 5s it is important to bear in mind that:

- Children have relatively high energy and nutrient needs relative to their size; this is needed for normal growth and development.
- They have small stomachs and immature digestive systems and may find it difficult to cope with large meals – small regular meals and snacks are preferable.
- Their appetites are not consistent and the amount they want to eat will vary; they may go through phases where they seem to eat relatively little or are insatiable.

In theory, providing the correct balance of foods to ensure a healthy diet is relatively straightforward. A healthy balanced diet should consist of:

- *Starchy foods* and *fruits* and *vegetables* – they should form the major part of the diet and be provided at all mealtimes.
- *Meat, pulses, milk* and *dairy foods* are protein rich, contain a variety of additional nutrients and should be provided on a regular basis.

In practice it can be difficult to be sure about the quantity of nutrients children are eating. In most instances it is not necessary – if a child is eating a balanced healthy diet the chances are that she or he will be getting all the necessary nutrients in the correct amounts. Considerable research has been carried out over the years to determine nutrient needs of children and adults alike. Box 1.1 explains the current position.

Starchy foods

Starchy foods provide children with energy, vitamins, minerals and fibre. Staple foods such as bread, other cereal based foods (rice, pasta and breakfast cereals), and

> **Box 1.1** Nutritional requirements explained
>
> The amount of nutrients we need – our nutritional requirements – vary according to age and gender as well as individual differences. It is difficult to be precise. In the UK the Committee on the Medical Aspects of Food and Nutrition Policy (COMA)*, estimated the nutrient requirements of different sectors of the population – *Dietary Reference Values (DRVs)*. There are four DRVs:
>
> - Estimated average requirement (EAR) – this is the average amount of energy or nutrient needed; by definition about 50% of children will be above or below the average.
>
> - Reference nutrient intake (RNI) – this is the intake that will ensure almost all (97.5%) children will receive sufficient amounts; this means that many children will require less than this value.
>
> - Lower reference nutrient intake (LRNI) – this is sufficient for only a minority of children (2.5%); it will not be enough for the vast majority of children.
>
> - Safe intake – in some instances there is insufficient evidence to set levels of EAR, RNI or LRNI and levels are set where there is considered that deficiency will not occur, nor is there a risk of consuming too much.
>
> DRVs have been set for various groups of children (and adults): 0–3 months; 4–6 months; 7–9 months; 10–12 months; 1–3 years and 4–6 years.
>
> *Now superseded by the Scientific Advisory Committee on Nutrition (SANC).

tubers such as potatoes, yams and sweet potatoes, are all good examples of starchy foods. Whole grain cereal products tend to contain more fibre, vitamins and minerals.

Fruit and vegetables

Fruit and vegetables contain vitamins and minerals as well as being another useful source of fibre. Fruit and vegetables tend to be high in water and low in energy (even though many fruits contain sugar). It is recommended that children eat at least five portions a day (two to four portions of fruit and three to five portions of vegetables provides a good balance). A portion for an under 5 is smaller than an adult portion. It is difficult to be precise but typical examples might be:

- Fruit – a small banana, half an orange or a whole satsuma, half a medium sized apple (sliced)

- Juice – approximately 25 ml diluted with water

- Vegetables – approximately 40 g (1½ oz) peas, carrots, sweetcorn, broccoli, etc. or a combination

Protein-rich foods

Protein-rich foods should come from both animal and vegetable sources. Animal sources include meat, poultry, fish and eggs. Oily fish such as mackerel, salmon and sardines are particularly valuable because they contain essential fatty acids and fat soluble vitamins as well. Good sources of vegetable protein are pulses – there are many varieties of beans and lentils and they have the additional benefit of providing starch and fibre. Unless a child is vegetarian, his or her diet should contain proteins from both animal and vegetable sources.

Milk and dairy foods

Milk and dairy foods provide children with energy, protein, vitamins and minerals. Full fat milk and milk products provide more energy than skimmed or semi-skimmed ones and are generally recommended for children. Children from two years onwards can be given semi-skimmed milk but experts advise that fully skimmed milk should be avoided until children are at least five years old.

Drinks

Drinks are important to prevent dehydration and constipation. Children are particularly susceptible to dehydration and drinks should be readily available. Water and milk are best between meals because they will not damage teeth. The acids in fruit juice can cause tooth decay – they should be diluted and be part of a meal rather than served on their own, to minimise the risk. Similarly, sugary drinks (typically sweet fruit or fizzy drinks) should be avoided between meals and generally provided in limited amounts – they tend to be high in sugar and acidity, which can promote tooth decay.

Meals and snacks

Foods may be provided as either small meals or snacks throughout the day. Ideally food provision should be planned so that meals and snacks are complementary and between them they provide a good balance of nutrients. For example, cereal and milk for breakfast might be complemented by some fruit as a mid-morning snack.

Processed convenience snacks that are high in fat, sugar or salt, such as crisps and confectionary, should be limited and provided only occasionally rather than daily. Healthier options might be: fruit (fresh or dried); vegetables such as small slices of carrots or celery; bread sticks, fruited cakes or carrot cake; cheese, yogurts or flavoured milk drinks.

Vegetarians

Children who eat a vegetarian diet should follow the same healthy eating principles as non-vegetarians but the sources of nutrients will, of course, differ. Vegans (who eat only plant foods and avoid any food from animal sources) need to be particularly vigilant to ensure they do not miss out on nutrients that are normally found in significant quantities in animal products. A vegan diet is at risk from deficiencies in: vitamin D, vitamin B_2 and vitamin B_{12}. Vitamin D is generated by sunlight on our skin; fortified margarine or spreads and fortified breakfast cereals are alternatives if a child has limited exposure to the sun, or has dark skin. Vitamins B_2 and B_{12} are added to some fortified breakfast cereals, and are present in soya foods and yeast extract.

Meat is a useful source of proteins and minerals such as iron and a variety of B vitamins. A vegetarian diet needs to ensure these essential nutrients are provided in sufficient quantities from non-meat or plant sources. Milk, cheese and eggs are fine.

Iron is found in many vegetables and pulses (beans, lentils and chick peas), in dried fruit (such as apricots, raisins and sultanas) and in some breakfast cereals, but it is more difficult to absorb iron from vegetable sources than from meat, so:

- Iron-rich foods should be eaten daily, preferably with foods high in vitamin C to improve the absorption of iron.
- Avoid tea or coffee as they can reduce the amount of iron that is absorbed.

Vitamin supplements

Vitamins A, C and D are particularly important in the growth and development of young children and drops containing these vitamins are often given to under 5s. It is best to get advice from a health professional before deciding whether to give them or not. It is essential that children get sufficient of these nutrients but too much vitamin A or D can be harmful.

The Department of Health recommends that, as a general rule, six-month-old babies who continue to be breastfed should have vitamin drops. Vitamins are added to formula milk and additional vitamin drops may not be necessary. Generally, all children between one and five should be given vitamin drops, particularly if there is a risk of deficiency – children who are poor eaters or have limited exposure to sunlight. Vitamin drops are usually available from child health clinics and are available free to certain groups.

Dental hygiene

The time at which first teeth start to appear is highly variable – around six months is typical. By the time a child is about 30 months he or she may have a full set of 20 primary (baby) teeth. The first permanent teeth appear around the age of six years.

Even at a very young age teeth can be damaged by acidic and sugary foods. Gentle cleaning should start when teeth first start to appear. Small soft toothbrushes should be used (hard brushes can damage the gums). No paste or a very small amount of fluoridated toothpaste should be used until the child can spit properly, otherwise the paste will be swallowed. Although fluoride is good at protecting teeth, children should avoid ingesting excessive amounts.

Be wary of . . .

Salt

Salt is naturally present in many foods. It contains sodium (a mineral) that is an essential part of the diet. The Food Standards Agency recommends no more than 2 g of salt per day for children aged 1–3 years (no more than 6 g for adults). Too much salt in the diet is associated with high blood pressure and related diseases. Unfortunately high levels of salt are present in many processed foods and it is easy to eat too much without really noticing – many snack products, ranging from crisps to instant soups, contain high levels of salt. If you rely on processed foods to feed children, try to buy the low salt options and read the labels – they usually give a guide to the amount of salt in a portion. Try to avoid adding salt to children's food (or your own!) during or after cooking. Children become conditioned to eating salty food and it becomes a habit that can be difficult to break. Prevention is better than cure – try to avoid giving children salty foods right from the start.

Added sugar

Sugar provides children with energy but it is not an essential nutrient – they can get energy from many other sources. Sugar can form part of a healthy diet although the amount of added sugar should be no more than about 10 per cent of a child's energy intake. In reality, it can be quite difficult to know the proportion of sugar in children's diets. It is not always easy to control the amount they eat because it is frequently added to (hidden in) processed foods. What makes it even more difficult is that sugar is often called something else! The scientific name for table sugar is sucrose but glucose (and glucose syrup), fructose, invert sugar, maltose are all types of sugar used in processed food. Then there are the different types of sugary products – molasses, treacle, demerara, honey, etc. which all contain lots of sugar. It is worth checking the ingredients in processed foods – you might be surprised at the foods that contain added sugar of one kind or another.

Sweet fizzy drinks and fruit squash often contain a lot of sugar – it is the sweetness that makes them popular with children. Squash should be diluted with water and consumed as part of a meal – water or milk is a better option between meals. Even fruit juice contains sugar (usually glucose) and, although they have the benefit of providing other nutrients, they should be drunk diluted as part of a meal rather than as a snack.

'Artificial' sweeteners are chemicals that have an intense sweet flavour and can be used in small quantities to replace sugar. Usually they contain no significant amounts of energy and do not cause tooth decay. Unfortunately, some of these sweeteners are known to cause hyperactivity, or have other side effects, in a very small minority of children.

Figures 1.3 and 1.4 compare the energy value of, and nutrients in, a few typical snacks. The examples have been chosen to highlight how the choice of snack can make a significant difference in the amount of energy and nutrients given to children.

High fibre diets

Fibre is a type of carbohydrate found only in plants. It helps children to maintain a healthy digestive system and prevent constipation, and should be included as part of a child's normal diet. In adults, the recommended level is in the region of 18 g per day but children should have significantly less, in proportion to their age and size. One rule of thumb is to add 5 g to a child's age – for example, a four year old should be eating in the region of 9 g (5 + 4). Too much fibre should be avoided as it is often associated with naturally occurring substances that can reduce the amount of minerals that are absorbed. In addition, fibre is quite filling and if a child eats too much, he or she will be too full to eat other foods that provide essential nutrients.

Animal fats

Animal fats tend to be high in saturated fats. Too much saturated fat in the diet is linked with various diseases and most experts recommend that children should eat only a limited amount. It is difficult to avoid some animal fats in the diet and, in

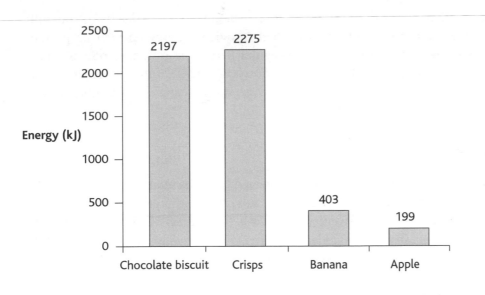

Source: adapted from MAFF 1995

The energy values of chocolate biscuits and crisps are much higher than the fruit snacks. The data refer to 100 g which is larger than a normal portion – a bag of crisps for example usually weighs about 28 g (about an ounce). The reasons for the differences are that biscuits and crisps are energy dense with relatively large proportions of carbohydrates and fats, as can be seen in Figure 1.4.

Figure 1.3 Comparison of the typical energy values of snacks per 100 g

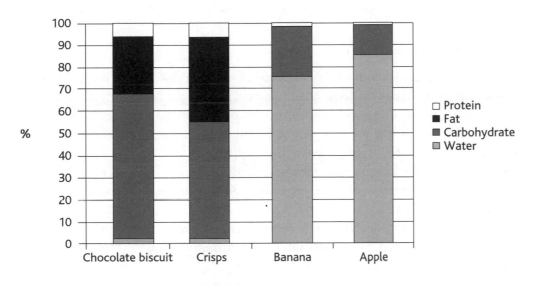

Source: adapted from MAFF 1995

Water (which has no energy value) is a major constituent in fruits and vegetables. Energy dense snacks have relatively large proportions of carbohydrate and fat. None are a particularly good source of proteins. They all contribute some vitamins and minerals (not shown in the chart).

Figure 1.4 Comparison of typical percentage of selected nutrients in snacks

moderation, there is no reason why children should do so. Indeed, full fat milk contains about 4 per cent animal fat which provides energy as well as protein, vitamins and minerals; it should form a regular part of infants' and toddlers' diets. However, foods such as butter, hard-fat spreads, cheese, fatty meat and meat products, biscuits, pastry and cakes are all concentrated sources of animal fat and should form only a small part of the diet.

Too much food

Children's digestive systems are not fully developed and the quantity of food they can eat is relatively small. Little and often is better than providing large infrequent portions. There is a temptation to feed convenience snacks between meals – crisps, confectionery, and so on, but these should be avoided. Children have relatively small throats and the risk of choking is much greater than in adults.

> **KEY POINTS**
>
> - Under 5s grow rapidly – they need the correct balance of nutrients to promote normal growth and development.
> - A healthy diet, which provides a good balance of nutrients, is based on a plentiful supply of starchy foods, fruits and vegetables and regular consumption of protein-rich foods from a variety of sources.
> - Small meals and snacks should be provided regularly; large meals should be avoided.
> - Meals and snacks should be complementary; keep snacks that are high in salt, sugar or fat to a minimum.
> - Vegetarians have the same requirement for a healthy diet but obtain their nutrients from different sources.

Find out more

There are many organisations that provide excellent and reliable advice, particularly:

Food Standards Agency (FSA) – their 'Eatwell' site has lots of useful information. This can be found at: http://www.eatwell.gov.uk or contact Tel: 020 7276 8000.

Another site that provides all kinds of useful information about child nutrition and more is 'KidsHealth' at: http://www.kidshealth.org

The Vegetarian Society provides advice and information about vegetarianism and healthy eating. They can be found at: http://www.vegsoc.org/ or contact Tel: 0161 925 2000 Fax: 0161 926 9182.

The Pre-School Learning Alliance is an educational charity that provides support for childcare including nutritional information at: http://www.pre-school.org.uk/food/ or contact Tel: 020 7833 0991.

The British Dietetic Association is the professional association for dietitians. They have a useful 'Latest food facts page' that has a number of fact sheets on food and diet related matters and can be found at http://www.bda.uk.com/ or contact Tel: 0121 200 8080 Fax: 0121 200 8081.

The Department of Health has a very large website covering a variety of topics including childcare and nutrition: http://www.dh.gov.uk

CHAPTER 2

Nutrients and their importance

Introduction

From a biological perspective, eating food is simply a way for children to obtain nutrients that are necessary for their health and wellbeing. After eating, the digestive system changes proteins, fats and carbohydrates into substances that can be absorbed and transported throughout the body. Then these substances may be:

- broken down still further to produce energy
- used to make new substances that are necessary for growth
- used to repair or replace damaged or worn out tissues
- deposited as fat if there is more than we need
- a combination of the above!

Children have systems and controls that work automatically to maintain the correct levels of muscle, hormones, blood, energy, and so on – all the things they need to grow and develop. They are remarkably flexible and adaptable and can cope with most situations, particularly in the short term. However, children's bodies cannot perform miracles and they need to be provided with the right sort of nutrients in the correct proportions if they are to grow and develop properly. Metabolism is used to describe all the chemical reactions that take place in the body and is further explained in Box 2.1. The remainder of the chapter considers the characteristics of different nutrients, what they do, and the possible consequences of too much or too little in the diet.

Proteins

Protein consists of hundreds of smaller units – amino acids – joined together in long chains. There are about 20 different types of amino acids that can make an almost unlimited variety of proteins. The variety is possible because:

- the total number of amino acids varies from one protein chain to another
- the proportion of each type of amino acid varies from one protein to another – each protein has a unique blend of amino acids.

This explains why, for example, muscle and hair are so different. Both are rich in proteins but the number and proportion of each amino acid varies greatly, giving

Box 2.1 Children's metabolism explained

Metabolism is a word used to describe all the chemical reactions that take place in a child's body. The food that a child eats, digests and absorbs is transported throughout the body to cells where it can be either:

- broken down to produce energy needed for all internal and external physical activity and maintenance of body temperature;
- used to build new cells or cell components and maintain existing ones.

These processes produces waste that needs to be eliminated.

Children use energy even when they are completely at rest. Normal functions – breathing, heart beat, maintaining body temperature, etc. – all continue and need energy. The rate at which energy is used when a child is completely at rest is known as the *basal metabolic rate* (BMR). Under 5s have a proportionately high BMR for their size, mainly due to their rapid growth and development. In addition to the BMR children use energy during physical activity – the more active the child, the more energy she or he will use. The *metabolic rate* is the rate at which total energy is used – a combination of BMR and physical activity.

them totally different characteristics. This variation in composition also explains why children should obtain proteins from different sources – overall they are more likely to get a good balance of amino acids needed for normal growth and development.

When children eat and digest protein the products are amino acids. Amino acids are absorbed and transported throughout the body to cells, where they are usually recombined to make new proteins or other important substances, such as genetic material. Normally, if children are short of a particular amino acid it is possible for their cells to make the type that is needed. However, this is not always the case – some amino acids, known as 'essential' or 'indispensable' amino acids, can only come from the food that they eat. This is another reason why children need to eat a balanced diet that includes a variety of protein sources.

What do proteins do for children?

Proteins are vital for normal growth and development. Proteins have a number of essential functions and are used to make:

- Muscle tissue, including the heart
- Connective tissue which joins muscle to bones and enables joints to function properly
- Skin (which has a protective function) and hair
- Blood that contains the protein haemoglobin, which is responsible for transporting oxygen throughout the body
- Hormones and enzymes that control our metabolism
- Immune system that fights infection and disease

Enzymes are worthy of further note because without them life could not exist. They are present in all living organisms and are responsible for controlling all the chemical reactions. In children they control digestion, absorption and utilisation of food. Without enzymes breathing, energy production, muscle contraction, growth and virtually all physical and mental activities would stop. Enzyme activity is not haphazard and children have in-built control mechanisms – hormones – that ensure everything functions smoothly.

Fats and carbohydrates are the prime source of energy for children. However, if these are in short supply or if there is an excess of protein, children can use protein as a source of energy. Excess protein may even be converted into fat and stored in the body, and may contribute to children (or adults) becoming overweight or obese.

Fats and oils

When fats and oils are digested the products are mainly fatty acids. Fatty acids consist of carbon, hydrogen and oxygen joined together in chains. Fatty acids can differ in:

- Size – the length of the chains can vary.
- 'Saturation' – fatty acids are said to be saturated when it is not possible to add any more hydrogen into the chain. Unsaturated fatty acids have some spaces left for hydrogen to be added. The more space there is the more unsaturated a fat is said to be. Polyunsaturated fats have lots of spaces where hydrogen can be added.

One difference between fats and oils is that fats are solid at room temperature and oils are liquid. A child's body temperature (in the region of 37°C) means that fats and oils are liquid inside the body. Fats and oils have a different composition:

- Fats – as a general rule fats have a high proportion of saturated fatty acids and the chains tend to be relatively long. They are solid at room temperature – animal fats and butter are examples of foods high in saturated fats.
- Oils – tend to be the opposite; they have a relatively high proportion of unsaturated and polyunsaturated fatty acids and short chains. Olive, sunflower and corn oils are good sources of unsaturated fatty acids. Oily fish – mackerel, sardines, salmon, and so on – are particularly good sources of 'essential fatty acids'. These fatty acids cannot be made in the body in sufficient quantities and need to be part of the diet (rather like essential amino acids).
- Hydrogenated oils – these are oils that have had hydrogen added to them. The result is that the liquid oil may become a solid fat. This is important for the food processing industry – hydrogenated fats have excellent cooking properties and are widely used in baked and fried products. Biscuits, cakes, pastry, fast food, snacks and some types of margarine often have hydrogenated oils as part of their ingredients. Hydrogenation often results in the formation of another type of fatty acid – 'trans fatty acids' – and there is evidence to suggest high levels could be harmful.

The problem with many foods is that they have 'hidden' fats – fat is often mixed or emulsified into foods and we are not necessarily aware that they are present. The eating quality of food – the taste but more importantly the texture – is often improved by adding fats and oils, and for this reason they are often incorporated into processed foods. Care is needed to limit children's consumption of processed food that contains high levels of fat. Low fat options are widely available these days but because of other ingredients (added sugar, salt, and so on) they are not always a healthy option.

What do fats and oils do for children?

Fats and oils are an important part of children's diets. They are a good source of energy, essential fatty acids and fat soluble vitamins. All children should have some fat and oil in their diets *but* (and it's a big *but*) too much fat or the wrong type of fat can have an adverse effect on health.

Weight for weight, fats and oils provide more than twice as much energy than carbohydrates and proteins. This is not necessarily a bad thing – a concentrated source of energy can be beneficial in young children. In terms of energy, there is no significant difference between fats and oils and too much of either will result in children having more energy available than they need. As a result, the excess will be stored as body fat and if this happens on a regular basis a child will become overweight or obese.

It is not just a question of the quantity of fats and oils in the diet, the quality is important also. There is strong evidence that too much saturated fat (including trans fats) can raise the level of 'bad' cholesterol in the blood and increase the risk of developing heart disease. The amount of saturated fat in children's (and adult's) diets should be limited but total avoidance would be harmful. In practice this means that animal fats (butter, fat on meat, many bakery products and dairy foods) should constitute less than a third of our total intake of fats and oils.

In contrast to saturated fats, there is strong evidence that unsaturated oils, particularly those which are high in the essential fatty acids, can help to lower blood cholesterol and promote good health generally. By lowering cholesterol and blood pressure they help to prevent blood clots and reduce the risk of coronary heart disease. Essential fatty acids may reduce the risks of other disorders including diabetes, stroke, rheumatoid arthritis, asthma, some cancers, and mental decline. Although the onset of many of these conditions does not occur until adulthood, their origins may start in childhood.

Box 2.2 Cholesterol explained

Cholesterol is a soft, fatty wax-like substance. It is produced mainly in the liver, normally in sufficient quantities to meet the needs of the body. Cholesterol is an essential component of cell membranes and the nervous system, and is needed in the manufacture of some hormones. In addition, cholesterol is commonly found in animal foods and they provide, therefore, another (unnecessary) source. Saturated fats in the diet are also linked to increased cholesterol levels.

The fatty nature of cholesterol means that it does not dissolve in blood. To enable cholesterol to be transported around the body via the bloodstream, it becomes temporarily attached to substances called lipoproteins. There are two types of cholesterol lipoprotein – low density lipoprotein (LDL) or high density (HDL). There are important differences between the two types.

LDL cholesterol is sometimes referred to as 'bad' cholesterol. LDL cholesterol can build up in the arteries (atheroma) and cause blockages, increasing the risk of heart attacks and strokes. High levels of LDL cholesterol are associated with increased risk of heart disease. In contrast, HDL cholesterol – the 'good' cholesterol – is associated with a reduced risk of heart disease. It removes excess cholesterol from the arteries and returns it to the liver.

It is a good idea to control the amount of cholesterol in the diet. The best way is to combine a healthy balanced diet with exercise. Foods that are high in saturated fats – butter, lard, hydrogenated oils – and foods that are made with these products – pastry, cakes, biscuits, – should be eaten only in moderation.

In summary

- Fats and oils are an important part of children's diet.
- All fats and oils are a good source of energy but they should be limited to reduce the risk of becoming overweight or obese.
- Unsaturated oils promote good health, and saturated fats (mainly animal fats) should be limited but total avoidance is unnecessary.

Carbohydrates

There are three main types of carbohydrate: sugars, starches and fibre.

Sugars

Sugars occur naturally in foods such as fruit (glucose) and milk (lactose) and form part of a healthy diet. Common table sugar (sucrose) is extracted from either sugar cane or sugar beet. Honey is virtually pure sugar and from a nutritional viewpoint there is little difference between adding honey or sugar to food. Pure sugar, unlike other types of carbohydrates, is not associated with other beneficial nutrients such as vitamins and minerals and for this reason sugar is sometimes said to provide 'empty calories'.

The main health problem associated with sugar is that it can cause tooth decay and can contribute to children becoming overweight. Children usually like sweet food, a liking that is often carried through to adulthood. In common with many people in the UK, children eat too many foods that contain added sugar which is often added to processed foods such as confectionery (sweets, cakes, biscuits, ice cream, and so on), fizzy drinks and a number of 'savoury' foods such as baked beans.

Fruit juices are relatively high in sugar and can cause tooth decay. However, fruit juice is still a healthy choice for children because it contributes vitamins and minerals to their diet. Ideally it should be drunk at mealtimes. There is a difference between eating whole fruit and drinking fruit juice. Most of the sugar in fruit is trapped in the plant cells and is not released until it reaches the stomach. The juicing process frees the sugar and juice is, therefore, another type of sugary drink.

Sugars need little in the way of digestion and children absorb them rapidly into the bloodstream via the stomach. (Diabetics have difficulty coping with rapid increases in blood sugar and the amount of sugar in the diet needs to be strictly controlled.)

Starches

Starch is found in plant foods. Children rarely eat pure starch (cornflour, used to thicken sauces, is an example of a pure starch). When children eat starchy foods they benefit from the other nutrients that are usually present. Starches are made up of thousands of glucose units joined together. Digestion of starch starts in the mouth and continues in the stomach and small intestine, and the product is glucose. Unlike sugar, starch digestion takes a little time so glucose is absorbed into our bloodstream much more slowly.

Fibre

Fibre is only found in plant foods. There are two types of fibre, soluble and insoluble. Good sources of soluble fibre are oatmeal and barley; legumes such as peas, beans and lentils; fruits such as apples, citrus and bananas; vegetables such as peas, carrots and broccoli.

Insoluble fibre (which used to be referred to as 'roughage') helps to maintain regular bowel movements. Humans are unable to digest insoluble fibre (we lack the necessary enzymes) and it passes through the digestive system and is excreted. Good sources of insoluble fibre are whole grain and foods made from whole grains (for example, wheat and rice), legumes (again), and many fruits and vegetables – skins and seeds add even more fibre (as well as usually being rich in vitamins and minerals).

Box 2.3 Energy explained

Children need energy to grow, maintain their body temperature, be active and maintain normal body functions. Energy comes from the nutrients in food – carbohydrate, fat and protein. Energy is produced in the cells.

The units of energy normally used in the context of food are kilojoules (kJ) and kilocalories (kcal). 1kcal is equivalent to 4.2 kJ. Carbohydrate (starch or sugar) provides 16kJ (3.75 kcal) per gram (g), fat provides 37kJ (9 kcal) per gram and protein provides 17kJ (4 kcal) per gram. A gram of fat provides more than twice as much energy compared with carbohydrate and protein.

The energy value of food is normally expressed as kJ or kcal per 100 g. The reason for this is that it enables fair comparisons between foods. Energy value is sometime expressed as kJ or kcal per typical portion which is useful if you are trying to work out how much energy there is in, for example, a bag of crisps or an apple. Portion sizes are often estimates because it can be difficult to know how big a portion size actually is.

The amount of energy children need each day varies. The Department of Health issues guidelines – Estimated Average Requirements (EARs) – for energy (and many nutrients):

Age	Boys kJ/day (kcal/day)	Girls kJ/day (kcal/day)
1–3	5150 (1230)	4860 (1165)
4–6	7160 (1715)	6460 (1545)

Ideally the amount of energy from food should match the amount of energy a child needs – there should be an energy balance. If too much food is eaten, the excess energy is stored as fat. Consistent overeating will result in a child becoming overweight or obese.

What do carbohydrates do for children?

Sugars and starches provide energy. After digestion, the resultant sugars are absorbed into the bloodstream and transported to cells throughout the body, where it is converted into energy. If there is more glucose than is needed it is converted into glycogen and stored in the liver, or converted into fat which is stored in the adipose tissue. Glycogen and fat can be used to provide energy at a later time, if necessary.

The rate at which energy becomes available for use varies according to the nature of the food. The rate at which starchy foods result in increased blood sugar levels is measured in terms of its glycemic index (GI). Foods with a low GI are digested and absorbed slowly, raise blood glucose gradually and are able to maintain these levels over a long period. Foods with a low GI are whole grain products, fruit and vegetables, beans and lentils – foods that are high on the list of a healthy balanced diet. Consumption of high GI foods results in rapid increase in blood glucose – most sugary foods fall into this category. High GI foods provide a 'quick fix' in terms of raising blood sugar but levels drop again quickly.

Insoluble fibre is plays an important role in maintaining healthy bowels. It absorbs water and increases the bulk of the waste matter (faeces), and the speed and ease with which it passes through the bowel. Balance is again important. Insoluble fibre reduces the risk of a number of bowel problems – some of them quite serious, including: constipation, haemorrhoids (piles), diverticular disease and cancer of the colon. However, too much fibre can interfere with the absorption of minerals such as iron and calcium, vital nutrients needed for children's growth and development. Foods rich in fibre are bulky and this reduces the quantity of food children are likely to eat. This can be useful in preventing overeating in adults but can have adverse an effect in children. They have relatively small stomachs and if they are satiated – filled up – with fibre-rich foods it may prevent other nutrient-rich foods from being eaten.

Soluble fibre slows down the rate at which sugar (glucose) is absorbed into the bloodstream and helps to prevent rapid changes. It also helps to lower blood cholesterol (which is associated with heart disease).

Constipation is a relatively common problem in young children and may be caused by a lack of fibre and/or insufficient drinks. A gradual increase in the amount of fibre in the diet in combination with plenty of fluids (water is fine) can help to alleviate the problem. Avoid sudden, large changes in fibre consumption – children find it difficult to cope and it can lead to painful wind and other upsets. At the other end of the spectrum, diarrhoea is quite common in the under fives. There are a number of possible causes – too many sugary drinks and fruit juice may be responsible, or too much fibre. Dietary advice remains consistent – give children a sensible balanced diet.

Vitamins

Children eat relatively large amounts of proteins, fats and carbohydrates. In contrast, vitamins are needed in only tiny amounts and are known as micronutrients. They are essential to ensure children's metabolism is efficient and effective. Children need them in the diet because they cannot synthesise them in sufficient quantities. Vitamins have specific functions – for example, many of the B vitamins are needed to help release energy during metabolism and a deficiency may result in tiredness or related symptoms. Vitamins A and D are particularly important in childhood development. Vitamin C is also important because it helps children to absorb iron. Vitamins A, D and C are often provided as vitamin supplements in the form of drops to children between one and five years old; six month old babies who continue to be breastfed may also be given vitamin drops. Severe deficiencies of vitamins can result in more serious problems such as blindness (vitamin A), rickets (vitamin D) or scurvy (vitamin C).

Vitamins A, D, E and K are all fat soluble – another good reason why fat should not be eliminated from children's diets (or adults). The B vitamins and vitamin C are water soluble. Table 2.1 summarises important characteristics of vitamins.

Table 2.1 The vitamins

Fat soluble vitamins

Name	Major sources	What does it do for children?	What happens if children do not eat enough or too much?
Vitamin A (retinol). Carotene and related substances are yellow/orange pigments found in many foods and can be converted into Vitamin A.	In animals, vitamin A is stored in the liver and it is highly concentrated in foods derived from liver. Dairy produce and eggs contain vitamin A. Carotene is found in carrots and many green vegetables – generally the darker the colour the more carotene is present.	Important for eyesight, especially vision in dim light. It helps to provide resistance to infections and keep skin and mucous membranes healthy.	A severe deficiency can lead to blindness. Deficiency can result in less resistance to infectious diseases and dry scaly skin. Excessive intake of vitamin A can be poisonous.
Vitamin D	Sunlight is the most important source – UV light causes the skin to synthesise vitamin D. It is present in low concentrations in some natural foods. Some foods, such as low fat spreads and margarine are artificially fortified with vitamin D.	Important in bone formation - facilitates the absorption of calcium, magnesium and phosphorus.	Deficiency can result in rickets – bone deformation that can remain thoughout life. Too much vitamin D may result in kidney damage – too much calcium is absorbed and is stored in the kidneys.
Vitamin E	Many foods contain vitamin E, especially vegetable oils, nuts, whole grains and seeds.	Helps to protect the cell membranes and ensure normal functioning of cells.	Deficiency is rare in children although it may occur in premature babies with very low birth weights.
Vitamin K	Most vitamin K is synthesised by bacteria in children's large intestine. Dietary sources include green leafy vegetables.	Helps to clot blood and heal wounds.	Deficiency may result in bleeding disorders and wounds not healing properly.

Water soluble vitamins

Name	Major sources	What does it do for children?	What happens if children do not eat enough or too much?
Thiamine (vitamin B₁)	Thiamine is widely distributed in foods – animal products, leafy green vegetables, grains and legumes. In the UK, white flour is fortified with thiamine. Cooking may destroy much of the thiamine content of food.	Controls the release of energy from carbohydrate during normal metabolism.	Deficiency is rare in UK. Extreme deficiency can cause a disease known as beriberi.
Riboflavin (vitamin B₂)	Riboflavin is widely distributed in foods, especially milk, meats and grains. Bottled milk may have reduced levels because the vitamin is destroyed by sunlight (UV light).	Important in respiration and release of energy during normal metabolism.	Deficiency in UK rare. Rarely occurs in isolation, usually combined with a shortage of other vitamins (see below).
Niacin (nicotinamide and nicotinic acid) – sometimes referred to as vitamin B₃.	Widely distributed in foods especially in meats and poultry, and wholegrain cereals. It can be synthesised in small amounts by the body from the amino acid tryptophan (see pyridoxine below).	Important in respiration and release of energy during normal metabolism.	May result in a number of symptoms such as fatigue, poor appetite, diarrhoea, irritability, and headache. Severe deficiency may result in pellagra characterised by dermatitis, diarrhoea, and dementia. Usually occurs with riboflavin deficiency.

Table 2.1 The vitamins (continued)

Name	Major sources	What does it do for children?	What happens if children do not eat enough or too much?
Pyridoxine (vitamin B6)	This vitamin is widely distributed in foods especially in meat, fish and poultry; some vegetables such as potatoes.	Important in amino acid and protein metabolism, and the conversion of the amino acid tryptophan into niacin.	Dietary deficiency is very rare. Dermatitis, particularly around the eyes, nose, and mouth. Very high intakes can damage nerves leading to numbness in hands and feet and difficulty walking.
Pantothenic Acid (a B vitamin without a number)	Widely distributed in foods, including animal products, grain, legumes.	Important in the release of energy from fat and carbohydrate during normal metabolism.	Dietary deficiency is extremely rare because of its wide distribution in foods.
Biotin (another B vitamin without a number)	Found in egg yolk, legumes, nuts and liver. Synthesised by intestinal bacteria.	Important in the release of energy from fat, proteins and carbohydrate during normal metabolism.	Dietary deficiency is extremely rare.
Cobalamin (vitamin B12)	Occurs only in animal products and micro-organisms such as yeast. It is absent from plant products.	Cobalamin works with folate (see below) in the production of red blood cells in bone marrow, cell division generally and maintaining a healthy nervous system.	Deficiency usually results inadequate red blood cell formation (pernicious anaemia).
Folate (folic acid and related compounds) – also a B vitamin	Widely distributed in foods especially dark-green vegetables, liver, nuts, and pulses. Also synthesised by intestinal bacteria. Easily destroyed during cooking.	Acts with vitamin B12 (see above).	Deficiency can result in another type of anaemia (megaloblastic).
Vitamin C (ascorbic acid)	Widely distributed in fruits and vegetables. Rich sources include citrus fruits, strawberries, tomatoes and leafy green vegetables.	Maintenance of healthy connective tissue.	Bleeding particularly around gums and under the skin; wounds do not heal normally. A severe deficiency is known as scurvy.

Minerals

Minerals, like vitamins, are micronutrients that are essential for good health. Some are required in relatively large amounts to develop and maintain children's skeletal tissue for example, whilst others, the trace minerals, are needed in only small amounts. Minerals can be classified according to function, such as:

- Constituents of bones and teeth – calcium, phosphorus and magnesium are important for normal development.
- Co-factors that help enzymes to function effectively – examples are copper and selenium.
- Components of other essential substances such as iron in haemoglobin which is essential for transporting oxygen around the body.
- Substances which maintain body fluids and cell contents at the correct concentration for normal metabolism – sodium and potassium are good examples.

Children do not necessarily absorb all the nutrients that they eat. One of the issues surrounding minerals is that of *bioavailability* – the degree to which the minerals can be absorbed and made available to the body. For example:

- Reference has been made to avoiding too much fibre in the diet. The reason is because substances associated with fibre (such as phytic acid and oxalic acid) can significantly reduce the absorption of calcium, iron, zinc and magnesium.
- Vitamin C, when taken with a meal (as orange juice for example) improves the absorption of iron from plant sources, and is particularly recommended for children who follow a vegetarian diet.
- Vitamin D improves the absorption and utilisation of calcium.

Table 2.2 summarises the important characteristics of minerals.

Salt

It is worth noting that sodium, found in common salt (sodium chloride), is an essential mineral. As with all minerals it is the dose that is important. Excessive amounts of any mineral can be poisonous and cause acute or chronic problems. It is generally considered that many people are consuming too much salt and this is contributing to cardiovascular problems such as high blood pressure.

Table 2.2 The minerals

Essential minerals

Name	Major sources	What does it do?	What happens if we do not eat enough or eat too much?
Calcium	Milk, cheese and dairy products are good sources. White flour (and bread) is fortified with calcium. Small fish where the bones are eaten (e.g. sardines and pilchards). Normally 30–40% of calcium in the diet is absorbed, the remainder is excreted.	Calcium, working with vitamin D, is vital for building strong bones and teeth. Heartbeat and muscle contraction depend on the presence of calcium. Calcium helps blood to clot.	Too little results in skeletal abnormalities such as rickets (bone deformation) and osteoporosis (fragile bones as a result of reduced bone density) in later life. Too much calcium may result in kidney damage, stomach ache and diarrhoea.
Iron	Animal products: liver and meat are good sources. Plant products: beans, nuts, dried fruit, whole grains, fortified breakfast cereals, dark green leafy vegetables. Iron from plant sources is more difficult to absorb than from animal products. Vitamin C aids absorption of iron from plant foods. Tannins (in tea) and fibre can interfere with absorption.	Iron is an essential component of haemoglobin, transporting oxygen in the blood to all parts of the body.	Iron deficiency can cause anaemia – typical symptoms include: tiredness, lack of stamina, breathlessness, headaches, insomnia, loss of appetite.
Phosphorus	Found in nearly all foods – milk and milk products, meat and cereal products are particularly good sources.	Important for strong bones and teeth, muscle function. Important in the release of energy in our body.	Dietary deficiency is unknown.
Magnesium	Widespread in foods. Magnesium forms part of chlorophyll, the green pigment in plants, and so is found in green leafy vegetables.	Important for strong bones and teeth and muscle function. Important in the release of cellular energy.	Dietary deficiency rare.

Potassium and sodium	Potassium is widespread in foods, particularly plant foods. Salt is frequently added to processed foods. Potassium may replace sodium in low salt foods.	Both are important in maintaining water balance, controlling the composition of blood and other body fluids, and for normal cell activity. Potassium is essential for the correct functioning of the heart.	Deficiency normally associated with water loss during prolonged physical activity typically resulting in muscular cramps. Too much sodium can damage kidneys in young children and is associated with high blood pressure later in life.

Trace minerals (these are essential but needed in very small amounts)

Name	Major sources	What does it do?	What happens if we do not eat enough or eat too much?
Cobalt	Widely found in food – good sources include fish, nuts, green leafy vegetables and cereals.	An essential part of vitamin B_{12}.	Deficiency can lead to a shortage of vitamin B_{12} resulting in inadequate red blood cell formation.
Copper	Meat, bread and cereal products, green vegetables, yeast, nuts, wheatgerm.	Copper is important to enable many enzymes to function, and for red blood cell formation.	Cows' milk is relatively low in copper and deficiencies may occur in malnourished infants.
Chromium	Good food sources include meat, egg yolks, whole grains, lentils, yeast and spices.	It is thought to stimulate insulin activity thus helping in the metabolism of sugar.	Deficiency is rarely a problem. Symptoms related to hypoglycaemia as a consequence of impaired insulin activity.
Fluoride	Widely distributed in nature. In some parts of the UK fluoride is added to drinking water to improve dental health.	Helps to develop strong teeth (and bones) and resistance to tooth decay.	Optimum amount in the diet is not known.

Table 2.2 The minerals (continued)

Name	Major sources	What does it do?	What happens if we do not eat enough or eat too much?
Iodine	Seafood (iodine is naturally present in seawater). Vegetable and cereal foods although the concentration varies according to the amount present in the soil where the plants are grown. Cows' milk in the UK.	It helps make the thyroid hormones. These hormones help keep cells and the metabolic rate healthy.	Deficiency causes swelling of the thyroid gland known as goitre. Too much iodine might affect the way in which the thyroid gland works leading to a variety of symptoms such as weight gain.
Manganese	Present in a variety of foods. Good sources include bread, nuts, cereals and green vegetables.	It is part of, and helps the functioning of, certain enzymes.	Deficiency is rare. Too much manganese might cause nerve damage and symptoms such as fatigue and depression.
Molybdenum	Present in a wide variety of foods such as peas, leafy vegetables, nuts, tinned vegetables, and cereals.	It is part of, and helps the functioning of, some enzymes associated with repairing and making genetic material.	Deficiency extremely rare in healthy people. The effects of too much are not fully known.
Selenium	Good sources include Brazil nuts, bread, fish, meat and eggs.	It plays an important role in our immune system and thyroid activity.	Too much selenium can cause brittleness in hair and skin.
Zinc	Widely distributed – good food sources include meat, shellfish, milk and dairy food, bread, and cereal products.	Zinc is involved with a number of important functions such as: formation of new cells, enzyme activity, immune systems and healing wounds.	Deficiency is rare. Leads to impaired development and decreased resistance to diseases. Too much zinc reduces the amount of copper the body can absorb and may result in anaemia and weakening of bones.

- Proteins are vital for growth in children; proteins should come from a variety of sources to ensure there are sufficient essential amino acids.

- Carbohydrates – sugars and starches – are widely distributed in plant foods; starches are usually associated with other nutrients and are digested more slowly than sugars, which should be eaten in moderation.

- Fibre is important but too much should be avoided as it can interfere with the absorption of minerals.

- Fats and oils are essential in the diet and are a good source of energy; low fat diets should be avoided but try to ensure that the fats are high in unsaturated and essential fatty acids.

- Vitamins A and D are vital for children's growth and development and for preventing infections. Vitamin C has a number of functions, particularly helping the absorption of iron during digestion. Supplements – drops containing these vitamins – are recommended for many children.

- Calcium is necessary for healthy bones and teeth; its absorption and utilisation depends on adequate amounts of vitamin D.

- Iron is important – iron from animal products is easier to absorb than from plant foods; vitamin C helps with the absorption of iron.

Find out more

There are many organisations that provide excellent and reliable information about nutrients, particularly:

Food Standards Agency (FSA) – their 'Eatwell' site has lots of useful information. This can be found at: http://www.eatwell.gov.uk or contact Tel: 020 7276 8000.

The British Dietetics Association is the professional association for dietitians. They have a useful 'Latest food facts page' that has a number of fact sheets on food and diet related matters and can be found at http://www.bda.uk.com/ or contact Tel: 0121 200 8080 Fax: 0121 200 8081.

The British Nutrition Foundation is a charitable organisation that promotes nutritional wellbeing and is an excellent resource, which can be found at: http://www.nutrition.org.uk or contact Tel: 020 7404 6504.

EUFIC – the European Food Information Council – provides a variety of information on general nutrition topics and can be found at: http://www.eufic.org

CHAPTER 3

Food choice

- What do children eat?
- Why people choose the foods that they do
- Hunger and appetite
- Sensory qualities of food
- Diet and income
- Eating trends
- Food and mood

Introduction

Under fives depend on adults – mainly parents and carers – for the quality of their diet. There are many factors that influence adult food choice and therefore the nutritional quality of children's diets. Even though we may know about the principles of healthy eating putting principles into practice is often ignored – consciously or unconsciously – by other more powerful influences. Research has shown that health is not the most important determinant of food choice and that there are many factors that impact on the food we eat and the food we provide for children.

At a basic level, food satisfies our hunger and enables us to function efficiently and effectively. Babies cry and young children can become irritable when they are hungry. Children have innate likes and dislikes of food and sensory properties are a powerful determinant of children's food choice. As they grow and become more experienced and discriminating, they learn to enjoy a variety of foods and reject those that they do not like. Children's perception of food will vary according to their physical state (for example, how hungry they are) and their psychological state (for example, whether they are happy, tired or irritable).

As children grow up their food preferences will become increasingly influenced by their social environment – family, culture, religion, peer groups, and so on. These social factors will continue to impact on food choices throughout their lives. When children grow up and become adults, their choices will have developed and evolved but their early experiences continue to play an important part in their diet. Creating conditions in which under 5s enjoy eating a healthy balanced diet will pay dividends in adolescence and adulthood.

Another important factor that affects the quality of children's diets is the economic status of the family. Links between education, socio-economic status and income have been demonstrated in numerous studies; families on low incomes tend to eat a less healthy diet. Not only do lower income groups have less disposable income, access to cheaper food sources are often more restricted. Low income families may have limited access to appropriate food preparation and cooking equipment, and this can limit the choice of food.

Psychological factors also play an important role in food choice. Bad experiences as a child, such as being forced to eat food she or he disliked, may be carried over into adulthood. Children (and adults) might associate a particular food with pleasurable or unpleasant events and this will influence our acceptance or rejection of food. Food is sometimes used as a reward or punishment. A child's acceptance or rejection of food may be a way of seeking approval or showing disapproval, or simply a reflection of her or his mood at the time. Children will go through periods when they have little interest in food, for no obvious reason.

Attitudes and beliefs about food will influence food choice. Debates over animal welfare, organic food or GM crops might be important for some. A family's religious or cultural beliefs may exclude certain foods or combinations. Some adults have no interest in food and consider it a necessary evil to sustain life. Whatever our attitudes and beliefs, the food industry and food retailers invest vast sums of money on market research and promotional techniques in an attempt to influence the food choices of both children and adults. They would not waste their time and money if the techniques were ineffective. Food is an ever popular topic in the media ranging from food scares through to the latest 'best ever', 'must try' diet! We are constantly bombarded with information about food and diet, often conflicting – who should we trust?

It would be easy if our food choices were simply a matter of following the healthy eating guidelines. The aims of this chapter are to investigate the ways in which children's food choice is and can be influenced and, given that adults tend to be the gatekeepers, the factors that influence our food choice.

What do children eat?

The National Diet and Nutrition Survey (NDNS), commissioned jointly by the Food Standards Agency and the Department of Health, collect information on our diets, nutritional status and levels of physical activity. The last major survey conducted on young children aged one-and-a-half to four-and-a-half years found:

- Sausages and dishes made from chicken, turkey and beef were the most commonly consumed types of meat products, eaten by about half of the children surveyed.
- Carrots, peas and baked beans were the most commonly consumed vegetables, again eaten by about half of the children surveyed; apples and pears were the most popular fruits, also eaten by about half the children.
- Twenty per cent of the children did not consume any fruit during the survey.
- Most children drank whole milk; the majority of children had soft drinks.

- Average intakes of B vitamins and vitamin C met recommendations.
- Average intakes of iron were below recommended levels and one in eight of the youngest children were anaemic.
- Vitamin A and zinc intakes were low in a significant proportion of this age group.
- Average intakes of added sugars were higher than recommended.

Although there is some good news (average intakes of vitamins C and B) there are some causes for concern. One in five children did not eat any fruit and vegetables. Iron (needed for healthy blood), vitamin A (associated with good eyesight) and zinc (a trace element needed for a variety of functions concerned with cell activity) are all below recommended values. In 2000, a NDNS report focused on young people aged 4 to 18 years and highlighted low intakes of some minerals, high intakes of saturated fat, added sugar (mainly from 'fizzy' drinks) and salt. Fibre, fruit and vegetable intakes were very low.

The findings of these surveys explain, to some extent, the results of other research that show that dietary-related diseases in childhood are increasing, particularly obesity.

What do people say are their reasons for choosing particular foods?

A recent European-wide study, reported by the European Food Information Council in 2005, was conducted to investigate consumer food choices; people claimed that the factors that were most influential were:

- Quality and freshness (the most frequently chosen)
- Sensory properties
- Price
- Health
- Family constraints (the influence of partners and children)

When asked about the influence of healthy eating guidelines, almost half the respondents reported that it had little, if any, effect on their food choices. Approximately one-third claimed to have made changes to improve their diets – over 70 per cent did not plan to make changes because they considered their diets to be satisfactory. The findings of this study highlight an important point about modifying eating habits. Evidence suggests there is a mismatch between perceptions and reality – people think they are eating a healthy diet when, in fact, they are not. It is difficult to improve eating habits of people who need to eat more healthily if they believe the contrary is true – dietary change is for 'someone else, not me'. If adults wrongly believe they are eating a healthy diet, it is quite possible that they are feeding children a poor diet in the belief that it is perfectly satisfactory.

Hunger and appetite

Hunger is a desire or need for food – it is a physical sensation that results from an empty stomach and depletion of nutrients in the blood. When children have eaten enough they are satiated and they no longer have a physical need to eat. However, children may continue to eat because their appetite is not satisfied. Appetite is influenced by social, psychological, economic and environmental factors. If children's appetite consistently overrules their biological need for food they are likely to eat too much or too little – their diet will become unbalanced. There are times when children 'lose their appetite' and they have no desire to eat; they might over-indulge on other occasions. It is important to keep things in perspective – children are quite adaptable and can cope with, and recover from, short term fluctuations in food intake. Problems are more likely to arise when children consistently over or under eat for an extended period. Serious eating disorders such as anorexia or bulimia are extreme examples of behaviour that ignores normal biological need for food.

Sensory qualities of food

Flavour

The flavour of food is a combination of taste and aroma. There are five tastes that are generally recognised: sweet, salty, bitter, sour and umami (a taste associated with monosodium glutamate – MSG – a flavour enhancer). Taste buds are located in various parts of the mouth (see Figure 3.1) and the taste of food only becomes apparent when we are eating it. Food contains many volatile aromatic substances. Each food will have a unique combination of these substances which, when combined with taste, gives food a particular flavour. Aromatic substances are detected by the nose and influence our expectations – either positively or negatively – even before the food is eaten. Food aromas can be powerful attractants or off-putting to young children, and will impact on their acceptance or rejection even before they have tasted the offering. If children are suffering from a cold, flavour is likely to be less intense and less (or possibly more) enjoyable.

At birth we have an innate preference for food that is sweet. Breast milk contains lactose or milk sugar. There is evidence to suggest that babies may develop a preference for foods that are slightly salty but have a clear dislike for sour and bitter foods. Foods that should be plentiful in children's diets, starchy foods and vegetables tend to be neutral or slightly bitter and so there is little incentive for children to eat them as a source of sensory pleasure. Fruits often have a distinctive flavour that may not be readily accepted although the sweetness of some varieties may encourage children to eat them.

Added sugar

Many processed foods contain added sugar, over and above the amount of sugar naturally present in food. The primary function of added sugar is to add sweetness which, for most children (and adults), makes food taste good. Confectionery – sweets, biscuits, cakes, chocolate and various combinations – are obvious examples of products with added sugar although it is added to many savoury products also. There is no doubt that many children enjoy the sweetness of these products and they develop a liking for them. As adults we can reduce our sugar intake by training our taste buds to prefer less sweet foods. Although food is less enjoyable at first, our palates soon become used to reduced levels of sweetness, and eventually many sugary foods become unpalatable. Children's taste buds can be trained also but there may be tears along the way! Infants are unlikely to appreciate the longer term benefits of reducing their sugar dependency; they may consider it to be a form of punishment! It would be best to prevent infants getting hooked in the first place but

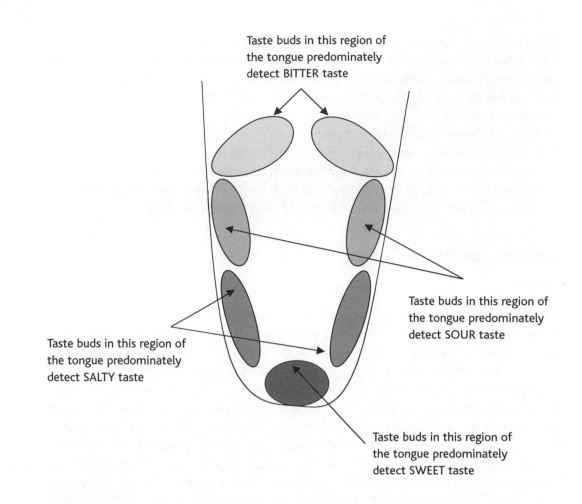

Taste buds in this region of the tongue predominately detect BITTER taste

Taste buds in this region of the tongue predominately detect SOUR taste

Taste buds in this region of the tongue predominately detect SALTY taste

Taste buds in this region of the tongue predominately detect SWEET taste

There are in the region of 10,000 taste buds. Most are found on the tongue (there are a few at the back of the throat). Taste buds are sensitive to only one particular taste and are concentrated as shown in the diagram. This explains to some extent why the taste will develop as the food passes over different parts of the tongue.

Figure 3.1 Location of taste buds in the tongue

this may be easier said than done. Figure 3.1 illustrates the carbohydrate content of some selected foods.

Salt

Salt is naturally present in many foods. Small quantities of salt, and the sodium it provides, are essential. Salt is added to food for a number of reasons, the main one being its role as a flavour enhancer – it intensifies the flavours that are naturally present (though often reduced during processing). Studies have indicated that approximately 75 per cent of salt in the diet comes from processed foods.

We get used to certain levels of salt in foods and a reduction may result in foods being perceived as 'tasteless'. We can train our palettes to eat less salt (in much the same way as we can for sugar). As far as children are concerned, it is best to avoid dependency in the first place – certainly avoid feeding high salt snack foods. Salt can be reduced by eliminating the addition of salt during food preparation, and never add salt to children's food after it has been served. Figure 3.2 compares the salt content of various foods.

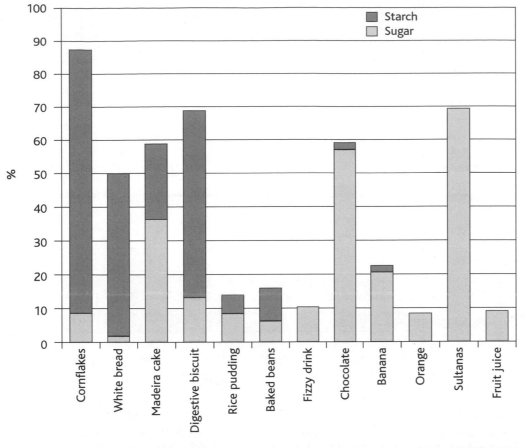

Source: MAFF 1995

This chart shows significant variation in the amounts of starch and sugar in different foods. Care needs to made when making comparisons as portion size will vary also – for example, sultanas are relatively high in sugar but only a few will be eaten at a time. Another factor that should be taken into account are other benefits associated with the consumption – fizzy drinks and oranges (and orange juice) have approximately the same sugar content but only oranges provide a variety of other nutrients such as vitamin C.

Figure 3.2 Chart showing the average percentage carbohydrate content of selected foods

Texture

In addition to flavour, texture plays an important part of the sensory experience, and fat plays an important role in food texture. It acts as a lubricant to help swallow food (for example, bread and butter) and is often incorporated into processed foods to provide an 'easy eating' experience – something many children enjoy. One of the many pleasures of chocolate is that it melts in the mouth – one of the principal ingredients, cocoa butter, melts at just below body temperature giving a smooth silky mouthfeel. Fats and sugar form an irresistible combination in many foods including cakes, biscuits, and chocolate bars. The pleasure of eating these sweetened foods with 'hidden fat' is countered by their potential for providing too much energy, sugar and fat in the diet. The problem is compounded because the fats used in these products are often highly saturated, which results in better cooking and processing properties.

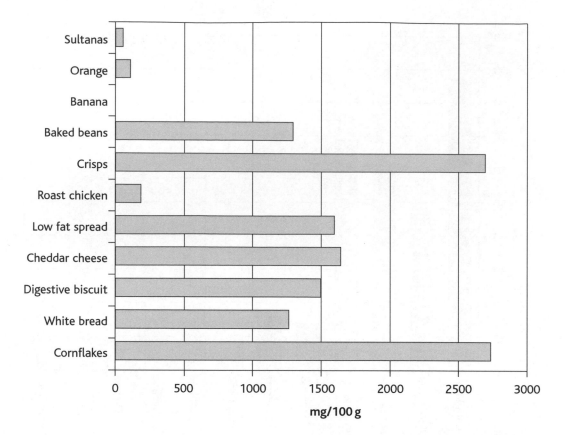

Adapted from MAFF 1995

This chart compares the average amount of salt in selected foods. The amount of salt is comparatively small compared to some nutrients and the weight is usually expressed in mg (milligrams or 1/1000th of a gram). 2000 mg is the same as 2 g – the Food Standards Agency recommends no more than 2 g of salt per day for children aged one to three years. Again, portion size is an important factor – 100 g is an awful lot of cornflakes!

Figure 3.3 Chart showing the average salt content in selected foods

Young children often prefer foods that are smooth or finely minced; they are easy to eat as well as tasting good. However, just because you cannot see the fat does not mean it is not there. Many people are not aware that convenience processed foods frequently contain high levels of blended and emulsified fat and they, or their children, simply enjoy the sensory properties that they impart to food. Figure 3.4 compares and contrasts the total fat content of selected foods, and the proportion of saturated fatty acids.

Appearance and sound

The appearance of food is important when it is on the plate – it gives visual clues about the pleasure it is likely to give. If children have had a bad experience of food, they are likely to reject it on sight if it is offered again. Children are often unwilling to try new foods (neophobia) and appearance may either encourage or discourage them to try it. Our sense of hearing plays little part in sensory enjoyment of food although there was a successful advertising campaign that claimed a certain brand of crisps was the noisiest!

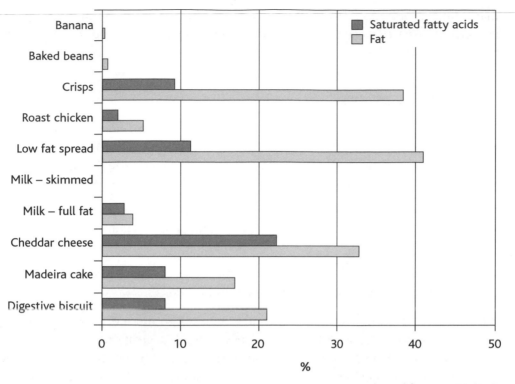

Adapted from MAFF 1995

This chart illustrates the wide variation in fat content in foods. There is nothing wrong with eating some of these foods as an occasional treat – they provide valuable sources of energy – but they should be eaten in moderation. Once again it is important to consider portion sizes and the benefits provided by other nutrients being present, such as vitamins A and D in low fat spreads and calcium in cheese.

Figure 3.4 Chart showing the average percentage fat in selected foods

Learning to like different foods

The sources of nutrients provided to babies and young children change rapidly. Before birth, the amniotic fluid is the source of nutrients that allows foetal development. Immediately after birth, breast (or formula) milk is the only source of sustenance. At weaning there is a transition to a modified adult diet with solid and finger foods gradually being introduced. Infants have an innate ability to learn to eat a variety of foods.

Sweet and salty foods tend to be readily accepted. Starchy foods and vegetables may be initially rejected. However, parents and carers should not give up too easily! Evidence indicates that infants will learn to accept food after repeated exposure. It requires patience by parents or carers to persist with offering food after it has been rejected a few times, but it is worth the effort. Acceptance is more likely if infants observe adults, siblings and peers eating the same food. It is important, therefore, that the rest of the family eat a healthy diet. A child might feel hard done by if he or she is being offered apples and carrots when the rest of the family or group are eating cakes and biscuits! Mealtimes should be social and enjoyable occasions although, for one reason or another, a child may refuse to eat anything. Parents and carers have come up with many innovative ways of encouraging children to eat, many of them borne out of desperation! In the end, and despite best efforts, children may simply refuse to eat particular foods at mealtimes. There is nothing to be gained by getting upset or upsetting the child – simply remove the food and try another time.

Diet and low income

Some of the main barriers to eating a healthy diet are cost of food and its accessibility. It is more difficult to provide children with a healthy balanced diet if they come from relatively low income families. Recent surveys highlight the fact that even though these families tend to spend a greater proportion of their income on food, poorer households consume:

- Less fruit and vegetables; salads; wholemeal bread and whole grain and high fibre cereals; oily fish.
- More white bread; full-fat milk; table sugar; processed meat products often high in fat such as burgers, kebabs, meat pies and pasties.

Fresh foods, including fruit and vegetables, tend to be more expensive than some cheaper processed foods. Fresh foods have a limited shelf life and there is an economic risk of having to throw it away. Research has shown that there is often a price premium on 'healthy' foods in low income areas. As a consequence, there is a greater reliance on lower cost energy-rich, nutrient-poor foods. This often results in the combined effects of under-nutrition (deficiency of vitamins and minerals) and over consumption (too much energy) resulting in children becoming overweight and obese. Poor diets in childhood may only become apparent in later life – research indicates that economically disadvantaged groups develop chronic diseases at an earlier adult age compared with higher socio-economic groups.

Access to supermarkets is important – estimates suggest that reliance on small corner shops and convenience stores can increase food costs by up to 25 per cent. Many people on low incomes do not have cars; supermarkets, particularly those sited on the outskirts of town, are not easily accessible. Car ownership amongst people in lower socio-economic groups is about half that of those in higher socio-economic groups and reliance on public transport is not always feasible, particularly for those caring for young children or who have mobility problems.

The level of awareness about the principle of healthy eating differs between socio-economic groups – a survey by the Food Standards Agency found that over 75 per cent of people from higher socio-economic groups were aware of the recommended '5 portions of fruit and vegetables per day' compared to less than 50 per cent in the lowest groups. Lack of knowledge or too much conflicting information on diet and health can prevent healthy choices. Lack of basic cooking skills inhibit buying and preparing meals from fresh ingredients, and the potential wastage associated with 'experimenting' or trying something new acts as a deterrent. Sometimes, there is simply a lack of appropriate cooking facilities.

Eating trends

As food technology has advanced it has become possible to manufacture an incredibly diverse range of food products – supermarkets have tens of thousands of product lines. It is debatable whether the food industry is creating or responding to demand for more convenience foods. There is no doubt that, as a nation, our lifestyles have changed significantly in recent years. Certainly our eating habits have changed and this has had a major impact on children's diets.

As a nation, we eat out more and many restaurants have a family friendly marketing strategy. Many 'fast food' chains provide convenience as well as an environment that is attractive to young children. Food tends to be relatively high in energy, fat and salt. There are sophisticated marketing techniques used to encourage young children to demand and eat more of these products – providing venues and catering for birthday parties is an example. There is concern also about the portion sizes that are served – these have increased over the years and, rather than waste food, it is often eaten 'because it is there'. A trend that reduces the opportunities for family meals together is 'eating on the hoof' or snacking either at home or while out. There is an opportunity for children to eat healthily on these occasions but it is frequently missed with crisps, fizzy drinks and chocolate bars being the order of the day. One of the biggest growth areas in recent years is the phenomenon of take-away sandwiches which again provides the opportunity to eat healthily (or not!).

There is a greater reliance on convenience foods in the home. Many adults lack the time, skills or motivation to prepare meals for children using fresh ingredients. People spend less time cooking now than they did 20 years ago – the average time spent preparing and cooking an evening meal fell from 90 minutes in the 1980s to about 20 minutes today. Convenience foods are not only quick to prepare but they often have a longer shelf life. The bulk and weight of fresh food, particularly fruit and vegetables, and the need to make regular purchases due to their shorter shelf life further discourages the use of fresh foods. In response to consumer demand, the food industry provides a range of 'healthy' meals, low in fat or salt or sugar, but care is needed because they may not be appropriate for young children. It is important to ensure that claims such as 'low fat' do not mask the fact that the product has a poor balance in other ways – high in sugar or salt, or low in fibre. Also, the vitamin and mineral content of convenience foods may not match that of the equivalent freshly prepared food.

The market for convenience baby and infant food is mature and there is a wide variety of processed food specially formulated for babies and infants. Most help to provide a balanced diet and provide a quick and useful source of nutrients in the early years. However, they should not be used for the exclusion of children sharing the same food with the rest of the family on a regular basis.

Nutritional knowledge

We receive information about nutrition and diet from a variety of sources – the media (TV/radio, magazines, newspapers), food manufacturers and retailers, food labels, friends and family. There seems to be an unlimited choice of books and magazines devoted to one type of special diet or another. The Internet is widely available and a search yields a wealth of sites providing nutritional information. Anyone can set up a website and there is no guarantee that any of the information provided is based on sound research and evidence – there may well be hidden agendas. Conflicting information causes confusion at best and can cause harm. Health professionals or reliable sources such as the Food Standards Agency, the Nutrition Society and the British Dietetic Association are the best options when seeking good up-to-date advice.

'You can lead a horse to water'… Although nutritional information and dietary advice is widely available, the extent to which anyone takes any notice is not clear.

Judging by the spiralling increase in dietary related diseases, its value in changing our diets seems to be limited and patchy. There is a great deal of current research investigating the best ways of effectively disseminating information about healthy eating, and bringing about changes in people's diets.

Food and mood

Food can be a powerful influence on the way children feel and, conversely, the way children feel will often be influenced by the food that they eat and the circumstances in which they eat it. All things being equal, children consume foods that they like and avoid those that they do not. A leisurely, relaxed meal with the family or carers can leave children happy and contented. By eating foods they enjoy, children (and adults) stimulate the release of endorphins – mood enhancers that make them feel good.

Children are prone to moods and their eating behaviour – acceptance or rejection – may be affected. It is worth noting food can cause a variety of reactions in children – the link between some food additives and hyperactivity in a small minority of children has been established for some time. The number of reported food allergies has increased over recent years and it is not just associated with processed foods. If you suspect an allergy or intolerance you should seek medical advice.

Attitudes and beliefs

Personal values, beliefs and life experiences will all influence food choice and the food that we feed to children. In the context of food choice we may be influenced by the way the food has been produced (factory farming/organic, multinational companies/local producers, fair trade, and so on). Our food choices will have been influenced by the society in which we grew up, including our religious and cultural experiences. Although our attitudes to food and diet may change as a result of new experiences and social encounters, our experiences in childhood will be reflected in our adult eating patterns and behaviour. This can, of course, be a positive or negative influence when we become adults responsible for feeding children.

The ways in which the food industry and food retailers promote food has a major influence on our choices and diet. The influence that promotional techniques exert has been studied widely, not least by the food industry and food retailers who are competing in a multi-billion pound industry. There is evidence that food promotion can affect under 5s' food preferences, food behaviour and consumption. A number of surveys have been carried out into advertising on TV, which show that the majority of food products are high in sugar, fat or salt or a combination of these. About half of all the advertisements screened during children's television are for cakes and confectionery. At the same time, obesity in children continues to rise and it seems that the healthy eating/lifestyle message is less effective than commercial advertising.

Food packaging is part product promotion – one of its functions is to increase product sales. Packaging is carefully designed to appeal to its target market, which includes children. Food manufacturers may seek to make their products even more attractive by seeking associations with cartoon characters (or at least from those organisations who have the copyright) and celebrities who will endorse the product. Although not part of the product, many offer free gifts to encourage children to influence the purchasing decisions of parents and carers.

The number of programmes devoted to food and food preparation on TV has increased over the years although the healthy eating message is neglected by most. Most programmes about slimming have a focus on entertainment or 'shock-horror' rather than providing healthy eating messages. TV is the most influential of media for adults and children alike. Various studies have been carried out on eating behaviour in fictional TV programmes such as the 'soaps'. Rarely does a family sit down to a meal, and if it does the meal is not finished. Eating is often a solitary experience and snacking on convenience foods is the most common way of eating. It can be argued that it is not the role of the 'soaps' or popular TV in general to provide healthy eating messages. Nonetheless, poor dietary habits are the norm in these programmes and they do highlight the difficulty of getting the healthy eating message across to children and adults alike.

Making changes

This chapter has highlighted a range of factors that influence food choice which, directly or indirectly, impact on children's diets. These factors are interdependent and cannot be considered in isolation – their relative importance depends on individuals and their circumstances. There is not a single message that will be effective for all individuals. The way to change children's diets is to influence the gatekeepers to children's diets (parents and carers) – it may be you! Change will only be effective when some of the other powerful influences on food choice are taken into account.

If you do wish to improve the diets of children in your care, applying the principles of healthy eating is a good starting point. However, the principles apply to the UK population as a whole and it is important to take due regard of individual circumstances, and bear in mind that there are differences between children and adults. That we should eat more fibre is a message to the population as a whole. A child who is already eating sufficient fibre does not need to eat more and it could be harmful. You need to take a thoughtful, pragmatic and practical approach to dietary change. Think back to yesterday – do you know how many grams of fat, sugar and salt you ate? Almost certainly not – it is difficult enough remembering what one has eaten let alone the level of nutrients that may have been present. We should not be too concerned with detail but should concentrate on making sure that the under 5s get the right balance of foods. Children do not have to like every type of food. There are no foods they must, or must not eat, and there are always alternatives. A common sense approach to eating healthily will be, for most children, good enough.

> **KEY POINTS**
>
> - Food choice is determined by many factors – healthy eating is only one motivation and, for many, a small one.
>
> - Children have likes and dislikes and will accept or reject food according to their sensory properties – it may taste good to you but children have their own opinion.
>
> - Low incomes can act as a barrier to healthy eating.

- For most people, feeding children convenience foods at home, in restaurants or take-aways is a normal part of life – they can contribute to a healthy diet but great care is needed because they are often high in fat, salt and sugar, and low in other essential nutrients.

- Advertising and the media exert a powerful influence on food choice and messages often conflict with the principles of healthy eating.

- Children's moods and eating patterns can be unpredictable, and can test patience to the limit!

Find out more

EUFIC – the European Food Information Council – have published an interesting document, 'The determinants of food choice' at: http://www.eufic.org/images/Eufic%20review_17_final.pdf

The Food Standards Agency has carried out research into food choices and the factors which inhibit healthy food choices. More information can be found at: http://www.food.gov.uk/science/research/researchinfo/nutritionresearch/foodacceptability/n09programme/

'Which?' the organisation that fights for consumer rights and campaigns to ensure consumers are treated fairly has interesting views on consumer food choice at: http://www.which.net/campaigns/food/choice.html or contact Tel: 0845 307 4000 or Tel: 01992 822800.

Diet and health

- Obesity
- Cardiovascular disease
- Diabetes
- Cancer
- Tooth and bone health
- Allergies and food intolerance

Introduction

The number of children with diet-related problems continues to increase and, in many ways, this is just the tip of the iceberg. Concerns about increasing food-related childhood illness now are equalled by problems that are being stored up for the future when today's children have become adults. Many diet-related problems do not have immediate symptoms and the effects of unhealthy eating habits can build up over the years. Food-related illness in adulthood may well have its origins in a poor diet in childhood. The situation is further complicated by the fact that it is difficult to establish direct cause and effect. Many diseases have a number of risk factors associated with them not just diet, and diet-related diseases cannot be considered in isolation.

Obesity is a particular problem in children and adults and many experts describe this illness as an increasingly severe epidemic. If the trend continues at the same rate, it has been estimated that as many as half of all children could be obese by 2020. A House of Commons Health Committee report in 2004 estimated that two-thirds of the population are overweight or obese; obesity has increased by 400 per cent in the last 25 years. Premature deaths resulting from obesity are estimated to be around 9000 each year. Approximately 4 per cent of young people are obese with a further 15 per cent classified as overweight. Obesity is associated with a number of other diseases and if it can be prevented, or at least reduced, it will have a significant impact on the health of the nation. Unless the trend in obesity in children can be reversed, diet related diseases will continue to be a major problem for the current and next generations.

Cardiovascular diseases – coronary heart disease (CHD), high blood pressure, strokes, and so on – are responsible for more than 20,000 deaths each year. The British Heart Foundation estimates that diet is implicated with a third of these deaths. Diabetes is a disease where blood sugar levels not adequately controlled – there are two kinds of diabetes known as Type 1 and Type 2. The number of people with diabetes has increased rapidly over the last few years – there are about 2 million in the UK. Type 1 is more rare (approximately 300,000) and it is the type that children are most likely to suffer from. Type 2 diabetes used to be associated almost exclusively in adults over the age of 40 – being overweight or obese is a major risk factor. Today it is increasingly being diagnosed in children. Cancer and diet have a strong association. Evidence suggests that around 20 different types of cancer are linked to diet particularly the stomach and bowel. Estimates vary but it is likely that about a quarter of all cancer cases are linked to diet. One cancer death in eight has been attributed to obesity – obese women have a higher risk than men. The risk of obesity-related cancer can be significantly reduced by changing our diets – the Food Standards Agency suggests up to about a third of cancers could be avoided by eating a healthy balanced diet. Healthy eating in childhood is where preventative measures should start.

Tooth decay and erosion is another problem associated with food consumption. In 1997, the Report of the Oral Health Survey (commissioned by the Department of Health and MAFF) found that nearly half of all children had some dental erosion by the age of six. The development of healthy bones and teeth is highly dependent on the quality of childhood diets, notably an adequate supply of minerals such as calcium and magnesium, and vitamin D.

Food sensitivity – allergies and intolerances – is a different type of problem that affects a significant minority of people. Although up to 20 per cent of the population claim to have a food allergy of some kind, current research suggests that in reality only about 4 per cent of children and 1–2 per cent of adults suffer from this ailment. Although in percentage terms this is quite small, in real terms around a million people in the UK are affected. There is some evidence to indicate that allergies and intolerances are increasing by about 5 per cent each year. Sometimes childhood allergies disappear in adulthood, sometimes not, and occasionally allergies can develop in adults when they were not present in childhood. Symptoms can vary widely from minor irritations – a mild itch or rash – through to severe illness and, in a few cases, death (about ten deaths a year in the UK are caused by food allergy).

It is something of a paradox that food is responsible for maintaining good health and yet it is a primary cause of illness. The aims of this chapter are to highlight some of the characteristics of dietary-related illness and disease, particularly obesity, and to discuss ways in which risks can be minimised in childhood. Specific illnesses resulting from vitamin or mineral deficiency have been covered in Chapter 2.

Obesity

Body fat

Body fat is essential for good health in children. Fat provides insulation necessary to maintain children's body temperature – children tend to lose heat more rapidly than adults because of their relatively high skin surface area compared with body size. Fat has a protective function– various organs such as the kidneys are surrounded by fat to prevent injury from bumps and knocks that occur in everyday life. Fat may be a source of energy during normal metabolism. At birth children have around 10 per cent body fat and this increases to around 25 per cent after a year. The amount of body fat can vary enormously – over 70 per cent in very obese people to less than 2 per cent in people who are seriously underweight.

Much of the fat is stored in tissue below the skin (sub-cutaneous fat). As the amount of fat increases there comes a point when children are considered to be overweight and continued deposition of fat results in obesity. Once children become overweight or obese the risk of associated diseases increases. In childhood, cells that are high in fat – adipose cells – increase in number and grow in size as a child becomes overweight or obese. These cells have a relatively long life and an obese child is likely to have more adipose cells when they become adults. The purpose of these cells is to store fat and so losing fat (and weight) later in life can be more difficult simply because there are more adipose cells.

Energy balance

Pound for pound children need more energy than adults – children have a higher metabolic rate and they need energy for growth. Babies and infants have only small stomachs and so a concentrated source of energy is important from a biological perspective. Up to the age of two, about 40 per cent of energy should come from fat in the diet. Approximately half the energy value of breast and formula milk comes from fat.

In the vast majority of cases, obesity is caused by an energy imbalance – too much energy (food) consumption and not enough energy expenditure (physical activity). Only rarely is it caused by a medical condition such as an underactive thyroid gland or an overactive adrenal gland. There are many risk factors thought to be associated with obesity in childhood. Research has shown that there is a greater risk associated with children:

- From lower socio-economic groups
- With obese parents or family history of obesity
- With parents with a sedentary or inactive lifestyle

Body Mass Index (BMI)

Deciding whether children are normal, overweight or obese can be difficult. There are variations in body fat due to individual differences in build as well as normal differences that exist between male and female children, and age. The Body Mass Index (BMI) is a generally accepted way of classifying adults. However, the BMI has its limitations and these classifications are not particularly suitable for children because normal growth and development cause rapid and significant changes in body shape, size and composition. Birth weight normally doubles by the age of six months and will have tripled by the end of the first year. The proportion of fat in children changes over time, and girls and boys differ in their body fat as they mature. Monitoring growth in babies and infants up to 36 months is achieved by using specially designed charts that compare body length and weight with standard measures. From two years onwards,

> **Box 4.1** Body Mass Index explained
>
> BMI is a measure of the ratio between height and body weight. It can be easily calculated by measuring height (in metres) and weight (in kilograms).
>
> $$BMI = \frac{weight}{(height)^2}$$
>
> For example, a woman who weighed 60 kg (9½ stone) and was 1.7 m tall would have a BMI of:
>
> $$BMI = \frac{60}{1.7 \times 1.7} = 20.8$$
>
> There will always be individual, gender and age differences so there are generally accepted ranges:
>
> - Underweight (BMI less than 18.5, some experts use a figure of 20)
> - Normal (BMI between 18.5 and 24.9)
> - Overweight (BMI between 25 and 29.9) and
> - Obese (BMI greater than 30)
>
> In the example above, the woman would be considered to be within the normal healthy range. The Food Standards Agency has an online calculator for metric and imperial units at: http://www.eatwell.gov.uk/healthydiet/healthyweight/bmicalculator/

BMI-for-age charts can be used – they are gender and age specific and take normal patterns of growth and development into account. If there are concerns about a child's weight or BMI it is best to seek the advice of a health professional who will be able to make accurate measurements and interpret the results correctly.

Effects of obesity on health

There have been a number of studies into childhood obesity and links with obesity later in life. There are some variations in the findings but it seems probable that something in the region of 40 per cent of obese children will be obese adults. As a consequence they will have an increased risk of:

- Heart disease and high blood pressure
- Type 2 diabetes
- Various joint problems such as osteoarthritis
- Increased risk of asthma

There are likely to be psychological effects on children who are overweight or obese, as well as physical problems. Children may suffer stigmatisation, discrimination and prejudice from their peers as well as adults; this can have negative impacts in both the short and long term.

Obesity and diet

If a child is overweight or obese steps should be taken to rectify the situation but they must be taken with care. Simply reducing food intake to lose weight is not a good idea as it might result in nutrient deficiencies that will interfere with normal development. Rather than trying to lose weight, a better strategy is to try to maintain a child's weight or allow only a slight increase over time as the body grows and develops. This will result in a gradual improvement in the weight to height ratio (BMI). In practice, this may be achieved by:

- Improving the diet by following healthy eating guidelines and Increasing physical activity – improving a child's overall fitness has benefits in addition to helping to control weight

It is not a good idea to single out a child for special treatment. Success is more likely if realistic goals are set, and changes in diet and lifestyle apply to the family. The chances are that the whole family will benefit from a healthier diet and more active lifestyle.

Cardiovascular disease (CVD)

Cardiovascular disease is a collective term for a number of conditions:

- Coronary heart disease (CHD) is caused by the coronary artery, which carries oxygen to the heart, becoming narrower usually resulting from of a build up of fatty material. The fatty material is called atheroma and the condition known as atherosclerosis. Atherosclerosis is a disease that typically starts in childhood. Narrowing of the artery reduces the amount of oxygen reaching the heart and might result in a painful condition known as angina. If the narrowed artery becomes blocked by a blood clot, this causes a heart attack.

- Strokes occur when blood vessels carrying blood to the brain become blocked or burst resulting in damage to the brain. Strokes often cause paralysis in the part of the body linked to the damaged section of the brain. In childhood, strokes are rare and are not diet related.

- High blood pressure, also known as hypertension, happens if the walls of larger arteries lose their natural elasticity and become rigid, and the smaller vessels become narrower. It rarely makes people feel ill but it significantly increases the risk of heart disease and stroke. If left untreated for a long time, high blood pressure can lead to kidney failure and impaired vision. As the number of children who are overweight or obese is increasing in the UK, the prevalence of high blood pressure is likely to increase in the future.

CVD and diet

A healthy balanced diet in childhood will reduce the risk of problems in later life. Research has shown that some foods have a particular influence in promoting or preventing CHD:

- Fruit and vegetables are thought to prevent the build up of atheroma in coronary arteries.
- Fats – the total amount of fat in the diet should be controlled in childhood and throughout life. Unsaturated fats have a positive effect on preventing CHD by improving the ratio of 'good' or protective cholesterol to 'bad' cholesterol in blood; too much saturated fat can have the opposite effect. Essential fatty acids

may help to reduce the risk of coronary heart disease and also to improve the chances of survival after a heart attack.

- Salt – avoiding too much salt will help keep blood pressure down. The UK Government's Scientific Advisory Committee on Nutrition (SACN) recommends the following daily salt intakes:
  - Less than 1g per day for babies aged up to six months old
  - Maximum 1g per day for babies up to 1 year of age
  - Maximum 2g per day for children aged between one and six years of age

Diabetes

Blood sugar

During digestion, starchy or sugary foods are normally converted into glucose, which passes into the bloodstream. The glucose is carried to cells all around the body where it is used for energy production. The concentration of glucose in the blood – the blood sugar level – is controlled by a hormone called insulin produced by the pancreas. People with diabetes are unable to control effectively their blood sugar levels and it results in too much blood sugar – hyperglycaemia. There are two types of diabetes:

- Type 1 diabetes – the body is unable to produce any insulin. Symptoms develop over a relatively short time – usually a matter of weeks – and the symptoms become very obvious. It is normally treated by insulin injections complemented by a controlled diet and regular exercise. Children are more likely to have Type 1 diabetes than Type 2.
- Type 2 diabetes – the body is able to produce some but not enough insulin, or the insulin does not work properly (known as insulin resistance). Symptoms tend to develop slowly and may not be noticed. There is a strong association between obesity and the onset of Type 2 diabetes. It is normally treated with lifestyle changes such as a healthier diet, weight loss and increased physical activity. Tablets and/or insulin may also be required to achieve normal blood glucose levels.

Effects of diabetes on health

Typical symptoms of diabetes are:

- Increased thirst
- Frequent urination
- Extreme tiredness
- Weight loss
- Genital itching or regular periods of thrush
- Blurred vision

Children with Type 1 diabetes can live a normal healthy life. Food needs to be eaten at regular intervals – delayed or missed meals can lead to hypoglycaemia – a decrease in blood sugar levels. The onset of hypoglycaemia in a child can be rapid and the warning signs can be different for each child but will be normally one or more of the following:

- Hunger
- Sweating
- Drowsiness
- Glazed eyes
- Pallor

- Trembling or shakiness
- Headache
- Lack of concentration
- Mood changes, especially angry
- Aggressive behaviour

If hypoglycaemia does occur speedy treatment is necessary to quickly raise the blood glucose level – if left untreated, the blood glucose level will continue to fall and the child could become unconscious. The child should be given something sugary such as:

- Sugary drink
- Glucose drink or tablets
- Fresh fruit juice

Once the symptoms have passed, some starchy food should be eaten to allow a slower release of sugar to prevent the level falling again.

Diabetes and diet

Although diabetes cannot be cured there are effective treatments to control blood sugar levels. Advice from a qualified dietitian or other health professional is essential. Most children with Type 1 diabetes can be treated by a combination of insulin, a balanced diet and regular physical activity. The principles of a healthy balanced diet does not change because a child has diabetes, it should be:

- High in starchy foods
- High in fruit and vegetables
- Low in fat (particularly saturated fat)
- Low in sugar
- Low in salt

The consumption of high levels of sugar, frequently an added ingredient to many confectionery and convenience products could be harmful. It leads to rapid changes in blood sugar levels that can be very difficult for diabetics to cope with. Specialist diabetic products have limited value and are no substitute for a healthy, balanced diet (neither the Food Standards Agency nor Diabetes UK recommend special diabetic products).

Cancer

Cancer is the growth of abnormal cells that grow and multiply to form tumours. Although there are about 1500 new cases of childhood cancer each year, food consumption does not play a significant role. However, in common with obesity and CVD, childhood eating patterns may have an effect later in life. Diet has been linked to several types of cancer including cancer of the bowel, stomach, breast, lung, prostate, pancreas, oesophagus and bladder.

Cancer and diet

The link between diet and cancer is complex. The Food Standards Agency suggests that what we eat could help us avoid about a third of all cancers. There is evidence to suggest that:

- Fruit and vegetables are likely to reduce the risk of many cancers, especially those of the digestive system.
- Red and processed meat (beef, pork, lamb, ham, bacon, salami and sausages, and so on) might increase the risk of bowel cancer. (This should be balanced against the benefits provided by the nutrients found in lean meat such as iron and B vitamins.)
- Fish may reduce the risk of bowel cancer.
- High-salt foods may increase the risk of cancers of the stomach and nasopharynx region (the area where the nose and throat meet).
- Fibre-rich foods (whole grain cereals and pulses, fruit and vegetables) can reduce the risk of bowel cancer.
- High fat diets can increase the risk of cancer, heart disease and other conditions. Too much saturated fat can increase the risk of breast cancer (but remember that some fat is essential).
- Vitamins and minerals could reduce the risk of cancer – folate (folic acid), selenium, calcium, and vitamins A, C and E are examples of nutrients that are thought to have a preventative effect.

The ways in which these substances work is not fully understood – it could be that a combination or 'cocktail effect' rather than individual nutrients are more effective – another good reason to eat a healthy balanced diet.

Tooth and bone health

Tooth decay

Tooth decay (dental caries) is becoming increasingly common in children. It is caused by a build up of plaque – a combination of residual food, saliva and bacteria – around teeth and gums. When the bacteria grow they produce acids which can dissolve the tooth's protective enamel coating, creating holes and cavities. Acids from fruit juices, fizzy drinks and fruit squashes (including sugar-free varieties) attack the surface of teeth and can cause dental erosion.

Sugary, sticky foods are the main culprits as far as tooth decay is concerned. Frequent snacking can also increase the amount of acid produced. Unfortunately, dietary advice recommends that children should eat meals and snacks on a regular basis! It is particularly important, therefore, that snacks do not contain the types of food that are likely to promote tooth decay and that drinks between meals should be limited to water or milk.

The most obvious symptom of tooth decay – toothache – indicates that tooth decay is at a fairly advanced stage. As well as ensuring a healthy diet, regular visits to the dentist, starting when the first milk teeth start to come through are advisable. As well as providing advice and spotting any potential problems, it helps to get young children used to visiting the dentist.

Bone health

Bones are rich in calcium, magnesium and other minerals. The absorption of these minerals is enhanced by vitamin D (the sunshine vitamin). Many foods contain calcium – milk is one of the best sources for children as it is easily absorbed. Bones are living tissues that grow in length, width and density during childhood and adolescence and bone density peaks at around the age of 30. Bone density starts to reduce as we get older and can lead to osteoporosis, a condition where bones become fragile and prone to fracturing. Building dense and healthy bones in childhood helps to protect us later in life. A 'bone friendly' diet is high in minerals, particularly calcium, and vitamin D.

Allergies and intolerance

Food allergies and intolerances are adverse reactions to the consumption of food that, for the vast majority of people, is safe to eat. Allergies and intolerance are not the same although the symptoms may be similar in some instances. Allergies are widespread in the UK, and it is estimated that approximately one in four of the population are affected at some time in their lives. Children under three years old are more likely to develop allergies than adults.

Allergies

Children's immune systems are designed to protect them from the harmful effect of bacteria, viruses and other foreign substances that can cause illness and disease. Allergies arise when the immune system mistakenly believes that a normally safe food (or other substance) is harmful. In its attempt to protect against infection, the immune system creates antibodies to the food. When the food in question is next eaten the immune system releases massive amounts of chemicals and histamines as a protective measure. These chemicals trigger a range of symptoms that can affect various parts of the body such as breathing and the respiratory system, the digestive system, skin, or the cardiovascular system.

If you suspect that a child has an allergy there are various tests that can be carried out to identify the cause. You should consult a health professional in the first instance.

Symptoms of an allergic reaction

The nature of the symptoms and their severity can vary, as can the time before the symptoms start to show. Common symptoms are:

- Coughing
- Wheezing and shortness of breath
- Dry, itchy throat and tongue
- Swelling of the lips and throat
- Itchy skin or rash
- Runny or blocked nose
- Nausea and feeling bloated
- Sore, red and itchy eyes
- Diarrhoea and/or vomiting

Rapid action is necessary if the symptoms are severe, such as:

- Swelling of the lips and throat
- Difficulty breathing or swallowing
- Collapse and unconsciousness

Emergency services (ambulance/paramedics) should be summoned in such cases.

Anaphylaxis or anaphylactic shock is a severe reaction to an allergy – it can be caused by not only food but by other things such as insect stings or drugs. In the UK and Europe the most common food-related causes of anaphylaxis are nuts, particularly peanuts, milk, eggs, fish and shellfish. When someone has an anaphylactic reaction, symptoms can occur in different parts of the body at the same time – any of those outlined above plus difficulty breathing, a rapid fall in blood pressure and loss of consciousness. Anaphylaxis can be fatal if it isn't treated immediately.

Allergy to proteins in cows' milk is fairly common in children and affects between 2 to 7 per cent of babies under one year old. The allergy can be caused by drinking cows' milk directly or indirectly via breast milk if the mother has consumed cows' milk or other dairy products. It often disappears as children grow – approximately 60 per cent of milk-allergic children outgrow it by the age of four and 80 per cent by the age of six (the other 20 per cent may remain allergic in adulthood). Typical symptoms of milk allergy are rashes, diarrhoea, vomiting, stomach cramps and difficulty in breathing. Symptoms are usually mild but in a small minority of cases milk can cause anaphylaxis.

Feeding children with allergies

It is an obvious but important point – take care when preparing food for a child with an allergy. Tiny amounts can cause an allergic reaction and cross contamination from one food to another can happen easily during preparation and storage. Equipment such as preparation boards, knives or mixers, or containers may have traces of potentially harmful substances.

Some food labels state 'may contain nuts' or 'may contain seeds' – these are food products that manufacturers cannot guarantee are totally free from small amounts which are sufficient to cause an allergic reaction. From 1 January 2006, food labelling rules will require pre-packed food sold in the UK or the rest of the European Union (EU) to show clearly on the label if it contains any of the following:

Peanuts	Fish
Nuts such as almonds, hazelnuts, walnuts, Brazil nuts, cashews, pecans, pistachios and macadamia nuts	Sesame seeds
	Cereals containing gluten (including wheat, rye, barley and oats)
Eggs	Soya
Milk	Celery
Crustaceans (including prawns, crab and lobster)	Mustard
	Sulphur dioxide and sulphites (preservatives used in some foods and drinks)

This list includes some of the more common foods that cause allergic reactions but it is not exhaustive – children (and adults) may be sensitive to other foods.

If you plan to eat out with children, always inform the caterers about any food allergies and seek assurances that the food or ingredient of concern is absent from the food, and that there is no risk of accidental contamination.

Intolerance

Food intolerance occurs because the digestive system does not produce sufficient quantities of a particular enzyme that is needed to digest food normally.

Gluten intolerance

Gluten intolerance or sensitivity, often called coeliac disease affects about 1 per cent of the UK population although some people do not realise they have it. If a child (or adult) is diagnosed with coeliac disease he or she must avoid the consumption of gluten – sometimes easier said than done! Gluten is a protein found in wheat and also in a number of other cereals including rye and barley. It is an important component of many flour based products such as most types of bread, pasta, pizza, pastry and cakes. Flour and wheat based products are commonly used as 'fillers' in foods such as sausages and cheap burgers, batters and coatings for many convenience foods, and as a thickener in sauces. Alternative starchy foods that don't contain gluten include rice, potatoes and corn. Gluten free products such as pasta and bread are available from many supermarkets and specialist shops.

Milk intolerance

Intolerance to cows' milk may be due to either a particular protein in the milk or lactose (milk sugar). Symptoms of milk intolerance can include eczema, vomiting, diarrhoea, and stomach cramps. Intolerance to milk protein is fairly common in babies and children but has usually disappeared by the age of five. Lactose intolerance arises because there is not enough enzyme (lactase) to digest lactose in milk and dairy products. It is rare in children; levels of lactase may reduce or be absent altogether in adults causing intolerance.

Summary

Diet, health and illness are all about probabilities and risk. It is clear that in recent years there has been an increase in the incidence of obesity, cardiovascular diseases, diabetes, cancer and tooth decay. Many of these illnesses do not show symptoms until adulthood although the seeds may be sown as a result of poor childhood diets. Attributing causes to these illnesses is difficult because there are usually a number of other contributing factors – lifestyle, physical activity, smoking, genetics, and so on. If children eat a healthy diet, there is no guarantee that they will not succumb to one of the diseases discussed in this chapter. Children may have a very poor diet and unhealthy lifestyle and live to a ripe old age! Nevertheless, the fact remains that the risk of illness and premature death is significantly reduced if children eat healthily, and continue to do so throughout their lives.

One of the reasons why it is sometimes difficult to get parents and carers to change children's diets is often because poor diets do not have a noticeable effect until later in life – it can seem rather distant and abstract. When caring for children, there are real and urgent everyday problems that have to be dealt with – long term concerns about diet and health might, understandably, have a low priority. However, if feeding children a healthy balanced diet is consistently ignored, children will develop eating patterns and habits that will be difficult to change later in life. Indeed, by the time the child becomes an adult the damage may have been done already. So, if we can encourage children to eat a healthy balanced diet, the risk of dietary-related illness will be reduced in both the long and short term, and more people will enjoy a longer and healthier life.

KEY POINTS

- Obesity is reaching epidemic proportions in both children and adults; it is associated with many other health problems.

- The diet of obese or overweight children needs to be carefully managed to bring about a better weight to height ratio (BMI) without compromising the intake of essential nutrients.

- CVD occurs as a result of poor diet over a long period, often starting in childhood.

- Type 2 diabetes is closely associated with obesity and this disease, which normally occurs in adults, is being diagnosed more frequently in children.

- The quality of children's diet can impact on the development of bones and teeth at a young age and the likelihood of osteoporosis in adults.

- The symptoms of allergies and intolerances can vary from mild to life-threatening, and occur in a small but significant number of children.

Find out more

Food Standards Agency (FSA) – their 'Eatwell' site has lots of general information about diet and disease. This can be found at: http://www.eatwell.gov.uk or contact Tel: 020 7276 8000.

The British Heart Foundation has been at the forefront of the fight against heart disease and provides valuable information at: http://www.bhf.org.uk or contact Tel: 020 7935 0185 or Heart Information Line: 08450 70 80 70.

Diabetes UK is the largest organisation in the UK working for people with diabetes and can be found at: http://www.diabetes.org.uk or contact Tel: 0845 120 2960.

Cancer Research UK provides a wealth of information about cancer in general as well as diet related issues and can be found at: http://www.cancerresearchuk.org/ or contact Tel: 020 7242 0200.

The British Dental Association is the professional body for dentists but some useful information is provided at their website: http://www.bda.org/smile/ or contact British Dental Health Foundation's Word of Mouth Helpline: 0870 333 1188.

The National Osteoporosis Society provides information on bone health at: http://www.nos.org.uk/

The Food Allergy and Anaphylaxis Network provides a range of information and advice and can be found at: http://www.foodallergy.org

Feeding strategies

Introduction

Some of you will already have experience of working in nurseries and pre-schools as part of your course and will realise that how children eat is just as important as what they eat. Physical, medical and psychological factors may all influence what a child eats, but these are outside the scope of this book and adequately dealt with elsewhere. This chapter takes a practical approach, examines the components of an effective feeding strategy and uses a series of case studies to illustrate different approaches used in childcare settings.

Successful feeding strategies

Successful feeding strategies are multifaceted and are best illustrated diagrammatically. Diet, appetite, the ability of the child to eat and the setting or environment in which food is eaten are fundamental to the success or otherwise of feeding strategies in childcare settings.

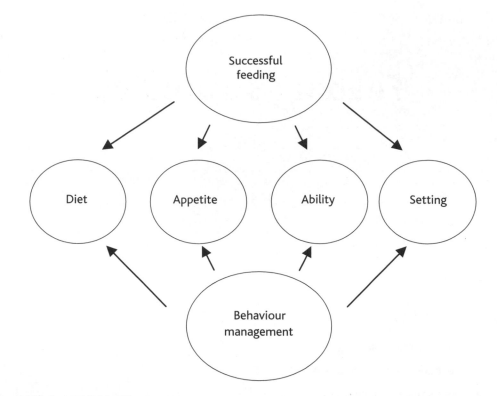

Figure 5.1 Successful feeding

Figure 5.2 Lunchtime at Charlton Nursery

Diet and menu planning

One of the primary aims of feeding is to provide sufficient calories and appropriate nutrients to support the growing and developing child. The food that is provided in the childcare setting may account for only a small amount of a child's calorific and nutrient intake, however it is important that what is provided is healthy, varied and representative of the variety of food groups discussed in previous chapters. It is equally important that menus are developmentally appropriate, namely the types, quantities and varieties of food are suitable for children of different ages. A strategy that incorporates repeated exposure to new foods and a variety of textures will help counter a child's resistance to new or unfamiliar foods.

Menu planning – what to include

This section is taken from information currently available on the Food Standards Agency website http://www.eatwell.gov.uk/agesandstages/children/yrtoddler

Between the ages of one and four, children are usually very active, grow very quickly and require plenty of nutrients and calories. It is important that food from the four main food groups is included every day.

When planning meals it is important to remember that although children can eat the same sort of food as adults, they cannot eat the same sort of quantities at one sitting. Meals for children under two should be packed with calorie and nutrient-dense foods. These include:

- Full fat milk and dairy products
- Meat
- Eggs

They should also be balanced by a selection of fruit, vegetables and starchy foods. You should avoid selecting too many foods that are high in fibre, such as wholemeal pasta and brown rice, as immature stomachs cannot cope with these foods and too much fibre may reduce the absorption of minerals such as calcium and iron.

Between the ages of two and five, children can progress to a more mature diet. This should be more bulky and include starchy foods, fruit, vegetables and not too much saturated fat.

What not to include

- Raw foods which are prone to contamination by food poisoning bacteria such as raw or lightly cooked eggs which may contain salmonella, raw meat and shellfish which may contain a variety of organisms which may lead to serious illness such as *E coli 0157*. All meat, eggs and shellfish should be thoroughly cooked.
- Whole or chopped nuts as they may cause choking.
- Fish which contain relatively high levels of mercury such as shark, swordfish and marlin.
- Salt – children under five should have no more than 2 g of salt a day. It is particularly important to check the labels on any processed foods that are being used to ensure that you are not exceeding these limits.
- Sugar should be avoided especially when it is contained in fizzy sugary drinks. Milk or water are better alternatives, and if fruit squash is offered at all it should be well diluted.

Vegetarian diets

You will come across some children who may be on a vegetarian diet. Particular care should be taken when planning menus to ensure that these children obtain all the necessary nutrients. They will require foods rich in nutrients such as milk, cheese and eggs, which will mean that their diet is not too bulky and they get all the protein, calcium, vitamin A and zinc that they require.

Meat is an important source of iron in non-vegetarian diets. Iron is also found in many vegetables, pulses, dried fruit and cereals. It is more difficult to absorb iron from vegetables so it is important that young vegetarian children are given:

- Foods containing iron each day
- Vitamin C in the form of fruit, vegetables or diluted fruit juices at meal times which will help them absorb vitamin C

Table 5.1 Food groups

Food type	Contribution to diet
Milk and dairy foods	These provide calories, protein, vitamins and minerals.
Meat, fish, eggs, beans, peas and lentils	These are rich in nutrients such as proteins, vitamins and minerals.
Bread and other cereals such as rice, pasta, breakfast cereals, potatoes, yams and sweet potatoes	These provide calories, vitamins, minerals and fibre.
Fruit and vegetables	These contain vitamin C, and other protective vitamins and minerals, as well as fibre.

Source: adapted from Food Standards Agency 'Eat well, be well' (http://www.food.gov.uk)

Food and culture

It is important to recognise that foods are closely related to children's family life and their cultural and religious beliefs. You should try and ensure that food is appropriate and familiar and that particular needs are discussed with parents or guardians. Cultural and religious beliefs are often related to food preferences and this may mean that certain foods may be excluded from some children's diets. Table 5.2 summarises the difference in food choice observed by people from different religions and cultures.

Variety

It is also important that children are exposed to new foods and textures. It is quite common for children by the age of two to exhibit a preference for certain foods over others or new foods. Parents commonly interpret this as a permanent dislike for a particular food and may permanently remove it from the child's diet. This may have the effect over time of restricting variety in the diet and in extreme cases exclude food types and important nutrients.

Table 5.2 Food related customs

Food type	Jewish	Hindu[1]	Sikh[1]	Muslim	Buddhist	Rastafarian[2]
Eggs	No blood spots	Some	Yes	Yes	Some	Some
Milk/yoghurt	Not with meat	Yes	Yes	Yes	Yes	Some
Cheese	Not with meat	Some	Some	Possibly	Yes	Some
Chicken	Kosher	Some	Some	Halal	No	Some
Mutton/lamb	Kosher	Some	Yes	Halal	No	Some
Beef and beef products	Kosher	No	No	Halal	No	Some
Pork and pork products	No	No	Rarely	No	No	No
Fish	With fins and scales	With fins and scales	Some	Some	Some	Yes
Shellfish	No	Some	Some	Some	No	No
Butter/ghee	Kosher	Some	Some	Some	No	Some
Lard	No	No	No	No	No	No
Cereal foods	Yes	Yes	Yes	Yes	Yes	Yes
Nuts/pulses	Yes	Yes	Yes	Yes	Yes	Yes
Fruits/vegetables	Yes	Yes[3]	Yes	Yes	Yes	Yes
Fasting[4]	Yes	Yes	Yes	Yes	Yes	Yes

1 Strict Hindus and Sikhs will not eat eggs, meat, fish and some fats.
2 Some Rastafarians are vegan.
3 Jains have restrictions on some vegetable foods. Check with individuals.
4 Fasting is unlikely to apply to young children.

Source: The Caroline Walker Trust (1998)

It is therefore important to recognise a balance needs to be struck when designing menus, between what children should be eating and what they prefer to eat. Repeated exposure to different food types, even though they are not always eaten ensures that children continue to have the opportunity to try items and see them as part of a typical menu.

Many children may dip in and out of the childcare and attend for the same session each week. It is important to make sure that they don't always eat 'lasagne' on Tuesdays. This can be avoided by rotating the selection of food available on different days throughout the year. Most nurseries appear to have a four-week menu which varies the days on which particular foods are served.

Appetite

Appetite is influenced by a combination of biology and environment. A child's appetite is often influenced by when and how often food is given. Frequency and duration of meals, are both important aspects of successful feeding strategies.

Figure 5.3 Healthy foods

Frequency of meals

By the age of two most children typically eat three meals a day interspersed with one to three light snacks. It is usual for children to show a great deal of individual variation in appetite; however three to four hours between meals is optimal for the majority.

Duration of meals

It is generally recommended that mealtimes last between ten and 25 minutes, depending on the number of courses and the extent to which the child socialises during the meal. Older children who feed themselves and socialise with other people are likely to take longer.

Short mealtimes (less than ten minutes) are rushed and may not allow a child to develop essential feeding and social skills. By contrast long meals, for example those over 45 minutes, suggest that the meal may be prolonged beyond a constructive point. This often occurs when children refuse to eat all or part of the meal. This behaviour is best ignored. Main courses and desserts should be offered as normal and food removed when the child has had ample opportunity to eat. Once the meal is over it is important that children who have refused to eat are not given snacks for one to two hours after, so that a clear distinction can be made between eating and non-eating occasions.

Figure 5.4 Lunchtime at Oaktree Nursery

Competence – ability to eat

The ability to eat is something which children will learn over time. To become independent feeders it is common for them to go through a period of messy eating as they begin to develop their co-ordination, use utensils and learn about the social structure of mealtimes. To this end it is important that cutlery, cups and other utensils are appropriate to the age and ability of the child. For children with physical impairments, adaptive feeding utensils can be used. Specially adapted feeding utensils can help children's success in feeding by regulating intake and keeping mess to a minimum.

Figure 5.5 Lunchtime at Charlton Nursery

Setting – organising mealtimes

The organisation and setting of the meal can be just as important as the menu. Research suggests that important aspects of the feeding setting include: physical surroundings, feeding position and body support, activities just before and after eating.

Physical surroundings: it is generally seen as good practice to provide an environment which is attractive, but allows children to concentrate on eating. This may involve restricting access to toys, television or other audio-visual distractions. Organising the eating environment, for example positioning tables and chairs in a consistent way provides a cue that it is time to eat. It is also important that any adults present are engaged in helping to serve food and feed children. Adults present who are, for example, cutting up paper for the afternoon cutting and sticking session, provide an unnecessary distraction.

Feed position and body support: a good posture during mealtimes, helps the co-ordination of children and encourages them to pay attention to their feeding. Most children up to 18 months will be secured in a high chair. As soon as they are able to sit still without wandering around the room, they will be able to sit on a suitably sized chair at the table. Most childcare settings use tables and chairs specifically designed for the under fives.

Activities before and after eating: the type of activities in which children are engaged immediately before meals may affect their behaviour during meals, particularly where approaches to discipline in the pre meal session conflict with those used during feeding. As an example, stimulating activities which involve a high degree of adult attention may result in uncooperative behaviour during meals. This is because of the change from a rewarding activity to one that may be viewed by the child as less rewarding. Also scheduling a preferred activity after a meal may encourage children to rush their meal or not eat enough. In the childcare settings that participated in the case studies many had a group activity such as story time prior to a toilet session and then lunch. This was followed by quiet time after lunch where children either took a nap or were encouraged to lie down on their cushions, listen to music or look at their own books.

Social interactions: it is widely accepted that it is best for children to eat with adults whether they are parents or carers. This is not normally practicable in nursery settings where most social interactions will be between the children themselves and the carers who are supervising or feeding them. It is particularly important that carers adopt appropriate behaviour management techniques which maximise the opportunity for children to eat the appropriate variety and quantity of food and drink.

Behaviour management

Examples of difficult behaviour commonly encountered at mealtimes include finicky eating, the refusal to eat certain types of foods and disruptive behaviour such as throwing food or utensils, throwing tantrums, screaming, being aggressive, stealing food from others, getting up from the table and eating painfully slowly. All or some of these behaviours will be exhibited in all children at some point in their early years. What is important is that they are managed in such a way that mealtimes do not become an occasion for open warfare.

Behavioural issues associated with mealtimes should not be viewed in isolation and may be linked with poor behaviour generally. They may also be inextricably linked with other aspects of feeding already discussed, so for example changing the setting may be fundamental to some aspect of behaviour management as may the provision of different foods or appropriate feeding utensils.

Stimulus control

The setting cues for eating need to be established and maintained. So for example only eating at the table and having a special mat or place name may help a young child recognise the cues, habits and routines for eating properly.

Positive reinforcement

For this strategy to be effective it is important that you 'catch good behaviour' and reward it with attention. There is a natural tendency to ignore good behaviour and focus attention, albeit angry, on poor behaviour. As far as a small child is concerned, attention is attention and it does not matter if it is positive or negative. For this method to be effective, reinforcers such as praise, treats and other preferred activities should closely follow the preferred mealtime behaviour. Table 5.3 provides a quick rule of thumb linking behaviour and reinforcement.

Table 5.3 Links between behaviour and reinforcement

Acceptable behaviour +	Reward =	More acceptable behaviour
Acceptable behaviour +	No reward =	Less acceptable behaviour
Unacceptable behaviour +	Reward =	More acceptable behaviour
Unacceptable behaviour +	No reward =	Less acceptable behaviour

Source: Herbert 1996.

Making undesirable behaviour not worthwhile

Example 1
Katie wanted to play with the dressing up box rather than eat her dinner. Mum said that there wasn't time to get the dressing up clothes out before dinner. Katie continued to nag and screamed at her Mum. Mum completely ignored her behaviour and continued to serve the dinner. Katie eventually calmed down and went to the table to eat her food.

Example 2
Katie was having her breakfast and kept throwing her food at her sister. Dad after one warning took the food away and put it in the bin. Katie screamed her head off and had to go to nursery without breakfast.

Behaviour that is reinforced tends to occur again. In Example 1 where the behaviour is ignored and example 2 where the behaviour is punished the behaviour tends to stop. It is important that rewards are not expensive, tangible things and that punishments are not hard or painful.

Time-out

In some instances disruptive mealtime behaviour cannot be ignored, particularly in a childcare setting as children commonly take their cue or get bright ideas based on the behaviour of others. In other situations there may be legitimate concerns for the safety of the child and others which may mean that the child may have to be removed from the situation. Time-out involves removing the child from the rewarding situation related to the poor behaviour or removing the source of provocation from the child. So, for example, a child may be removed to a time-out area or stool in the corner or the food that he/she has been throwing is removed.

To be effective time-out should be applied:

● Consistently, whenever the undesirable behaviour occurs
● Immediately after the event so that the child associates their undesirable behaviour with the consequences
● With minimum attention
● For short supervised period of time two to five minutes
● In conjunction with praise for good behaviour

Of course this mild form of punishment may backfire particularly if the child is happy to be removed from the meal. The success of time-out depends on:

● The time-out situation being boring, no reward interest or stimulation.
● The situation from which the child is being removed being rewarding.
● The reward value of the food that is removed. This will depend on a child's appetite and food preferences.

Using natural consequences

This method may be more effective with older children, although it would probably be used more commonly in the home than in a childcare setting. Clearly children cannot be forced to eat at mealtimes, however you can have control over what they eat in between meals. Children who do not eat will get hungry and this can be used advantageously. It may be possible to explain that if the child has not eaten their meal within a certain time then it will be taken away and there will be nothing to eat until the next meal. This establishes mealtimes as the primary eating events during the day.

These are the common interventions that may be employed in nursery settings. Others may require the intervention of psychologists and health care professionals and are outside the scope of this text.

Food and curriculum

Children's understanding of food is best achieved by embedding it in the curriculum and not teaching it as an isolated subject. Ofsted suggest that food and nutrition education can be used as a vehicle to:

- Have a wide range of first hand experiences, with appropriate interventions by the staff to extend and develop the learning that is taking place
- Take part in activities that build on and extend their interests, capabilities and experiences
- Have opportunities to be imaginative and creative
- Learn to interact and communicate with others
- Become increasingly independent and develop a sense of wellbeing and achievement
- Show initiative and become increasingly independent and responsible for themselves and their actions
- Develop physical skills

(Ofsted July 2004)

One approach and one that was reported in Ofsted (2004) looked at the competences that a nursery were seeking to develop.

Example 1: taken from Ofsted (2004)

In a nursery, the staff have decided that it is important for the children to be able to:

- Name a range of foods
- Understand that similar foods can be grouped, for example as fruit and vegetables
- Appreciate that foods in the same group have different characteristics such as tastes
- Express their likes and dislikes
- Begin to understand that different foods come in a variety of different forms

The task today is to look at different fruits. A group of three year old children work with their teacher, watching as she dissects four different types of fruit to show their various structures and to highlight particular features, such as what the skin looks like, what colour the flesh is and whether there are pips and seeds. She encourages them to taste the food and to give their opinions on whether they like it or not. She comments carefully on what they say, extending their vocabulary in doing so and encouraging them to look for other features in each piece of fruit, such as whether it is juicy or not. She also has a commercial fruit bar, containing 48 per cent fruit, that is made up of the same set of fruits that the children are tasting. She encourages the children to compare the taste and appearance of the bar with the fresh fruits. The children are thoroughly absorbed, helped by their teacher's considerable expertise in encouraging them to sample the foods and to observe closely. They do this willingly and intently. This is a very powerful session in promoting their understanding and helping them to develop their competences.

Resources

One of the best resources, and based upon the British diet is 'the balance of good health' which is used by the Food Standards Agency.

This divides a dinner plate into five sections with different food groups in each section. It provides a useful basis for healthy eating by helping children to understand;

● The concept of a healthy diet

● The proportion of food that should be eaten from each food group

● That a healthy diet is composed of foods eaten over a period of time

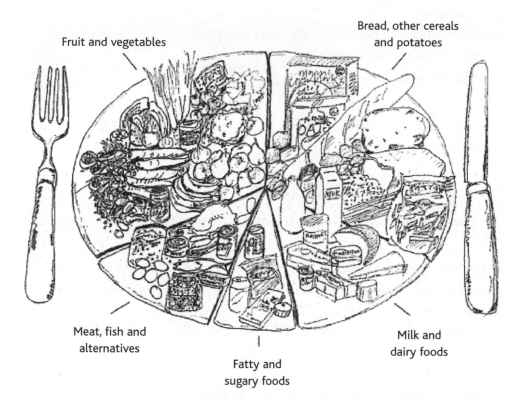

The 'Balance of good health' plate from the Grab 5! Curriculum Pack. Reproduced by kind permission of Sustain (http://www.sustainweb.org).

Figure 5.6 The 'balance of good health' plate

Mealtimes

Mealtimes in childcare settings also give children the opportunity to learn about food. In some childcare settings it is common for children to help prepare simple snacks such as fruit, lay tables, serve themselves and younger children, and clear away. It is essential that the food children receive is healthy and that they know the difference between healthy and unhealthy foods.

Food and play

It is also important that food is integrated into play. Role-play including activities such as shopping, preparing and eating food are all part of a child's development. Many childcare settings also involve children in simple cooking activities such as making cakes, biscuits and pizzas. This gives them a sense of satisfaction and sensory pleasure as they see the changes that take place during preparation and cooking. Children always enjoy these activities and they learn a lot about the smell, taste and texture of the food that they are handling. Although most nurseries do not have specialist food preparation rooms, generalist facilities can be used as long as they are managed carefully to ensure that the area is safe and hygienic and that all children and staff wash their hands effectively before handling food.

Figure 5.7 Food and play at Charlton Nursery

Figure 5.8 Food and play at Oak Tree Nursery

Case study 1: Oak Tree Day Nursery

Profile

Oak Tree Day Nursery is attached to a university and provides childcare to staff, students and people in the nearby community. Twenty-seven children attend the nursery on any one day and there are a total of 39 children who attend over the course of the week on a daily or sessional basis. Ages vary between six months and five years. The under twos are housed and eat in a separate building. This case study focuses on the feeding strategies adopted for those children aged between two and five. Oak Tree Day Nursery provides three meals a day, a morning and afternoon snack and a midday meal. Where children are dropped off early (before 8.30 am) or picked up (after 5.30 pm), parents bring along breakfast or other meals which are given to them before or after the main nursery day. These children are in the minority and number one or two maximum on any given day.

Preparation

The lunchtime meal is prepared in the main university kitchen and delivered before lunch. The food for morning and afternoon snacks is bought by the nursery staff and freshly prepared by one of them before the morning and afternoon snack time.

Menu planning

For the last two years menus have been planned by the nursery manager, based on good nutritional practice, and what children are most likely to eat. The manager derived her information from a variety of recipe and childcare books which focus on the under fives. Prior to this the lunchtime menu was decided by the main kitchen. A number of issues prompted a shift in responsibility. These included instances where unhealthy food such as chicken teddies or food that children found challenging or unacceptable were included on the menu. A number of foods are specifically excluded from the menu. These tend to be foods which are unhealthy or children may be allergic to. These include eggs, nuts and processed meats. There is a specific request that no salt is used in preparation, and that where processed foods are used that salt levels on labels are checked carefully.

The menu is designed to rotate over a four week cycle and ensures that within this different foods are provided on different days.

Special dietary requests

Vegetarian and vegan options are available. Any other special requests are discussed with parents on a one-to-one basis and are accommodated where possible.

Food choice

Food choice is limited. However children are asked what they would like on their plate. They are encouraged to eat the full range of food available, but staff are sensitive to likes and dislikes. Children are not forced to eat foods that they find unacceptable and dessert is not used as a reward for a 'clean plate'.

Parents' influence on food choice

The parents at Oak Tree have limited input into the menu. It is available to them on request and displayed in the nursery. Daily reporting either through day books or on the noticeboard ensures that for the younger children (under threes) parents know the food type and quantity consumed by their child and for the older children the noticeboard indicates whether or not they have eaten their food.

Scheduling

The children at Oak Tree are offered three meals a day.

- A snack at 10.30 am which comprises a selection of fruit and either milk or water
- A more substantial snack at 3.30 pm of sandwiches or toast and water or milk to drink
- A two course lunch at 12.30 with water to drink

Immediately before all snacks and meals, children help to tidy up their last activity and then use the toilet and wash their hands. The morning snack is preceded by a creative activity and in the afternoon it is preceded by circle time. Lunch is preceded by outdoor play and immediately followed by quiet time. Snack time usually lasts about 20 minutes and lunch 30–45 minutes. There is no formal policy about meal length as the staff believe that meals should be a social occasion where children interact with each other and their carers. Individual requests for additional food and drink are assessed on a case-by-case basis. Water is freely available and children are encouraged to drink more on hot days and when they have been doing an energetic activity.

Environment

Children eat their meals and snacks at the table in an area separate from the main play area. The older children are given the responsibility for simple chores such as setting out the name plates, putting out the cups. They are also encouraged to pour their own drinks. These chores are decided on a daily basis by staff and older children at circle time.

The staff do not eat with the children as resources and space are limited. The nursery manager did admit that if resources allowed she would encourage this practice.

Utensils

A range of utensils is provided which are suitable for the ages and abilities of the children. They are encouraged to use utensils appropriately but not to the exclusion of eating their food. Using fingers, and so on, is acceptable. For children who are particularly fussy or phobic, the nursery may suggest that the child brings in their own cup, plate and utensils.

Behavioural issues

Oak Tree adopts a positive reinforcement policy to all behavioural issues. If a particular undesirable behaviour cannot be discouraged using this method, supervised time-out may be used.

Children who are fussy eaters and exhibit phobias about food are encouraged to choose a variety of foods. However, where a child displays a particular dislike for a food then it would not be put on their plate. Playing with food is tolerated particularly among the younger children. However, as they get older, this is discouraged.

If children are particularly slow at eating, then they are allowed to continue at their own pace but others would be allowed to leave the table.

Other unacceptable behaviour such as throwing food, tantrums or stealing food from others, would be dealt with by explaining the consequences of the particular behaviour. In extreme cases supervised time-out would be used, particularly if the undesirable behaviour continued after repeated warnings.

Food and play

The children at Oak Tree are encouraged to participate in cooking activities, even the babies do it! They participate typically in making simple foods such as pizza, biscuits and chocolate crispie cake, which they then eat for their afternoon snack. They are also encouraged to role-play. There is a cooking corner and a food stall for them to play shop.

Food and the curriculum

Oak Tree meets the early learning goals of the national curriculum. Children learn about healthy food and balanced diets as part of being healthy.

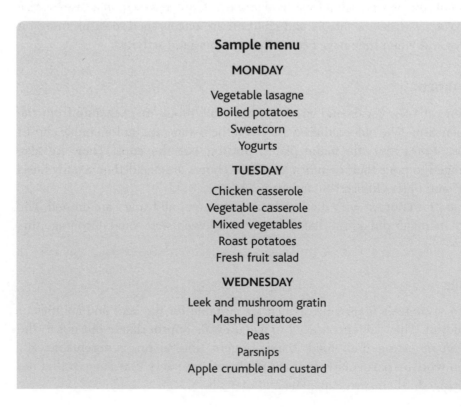

Sample menu

MONDAY

Vegetable lasagne
Boiled potatoes
Sweetcorn
Yogurts

TUESDAY

Chicken casserole
Vegetable casserole
Mixed vegetables
Roast potatoes
Fresh fruit salad

WEDNESDAY

Leek and mushroom gratin
Mashed potatoes
Peas
Parsnips
Apple crumble and custard

THURSDAY

Roast lamb

Roasted vegetable risotto

Broccoli

Swede

Roast potatoes

Jam sponge and custard

FRIDAY

Fish pie

Vegetable stroganoff with rice

Peas

Banana custard

Morning snacks are always a selection of fruit and milk or water to drink.

Afternoon snacks are always savoury/sweet sandwiches or toast with water or milk to drink.

Water is offered as a drink with the main lunchtime meal.

Case study 2: Charlton Nursery

Profile

Charlton Nursery is an independent nursery providing childcare for members of the local community. It is registered for up to 75 children between the ages of six weeks and six years. There are a total of 69 children who attend over the course of a week on a daily or sessional basis. Children are housed in different parts of the building according to age and eat in their respective age groups: babies aged six weeks to 14 months in the Snowdrop Room; toddlers 14 months to 30 months in the Daffodil Room; children two-and-a-half to three-and-a-half years in the Bluebell Room and children aged three-and-a-half to four-and-a-half in the Pre-school room. This case study focuses on the provision of food and feeding strategies adopted for those children aged between two-and-a-half and five. Charlton Nursery provides four meals a day depending on when children are dropped off or picked up by their parents. Good food is central to the childcare policy at Charlton and in fact many parents choose this nursery because of the diet which is healthy, nutritious and uses fresh, and where possible organic and local ingredients.

Food preparation

All food is prepared in the main kitchen which is located in the centre of the nursery. It is prepared, placed into trays and taken to the rooms in which the children eat their meals. The kitchen is readily accessible and can be seen by the children when they arrive at, and move around the nursery. The directors of the nursery are keen to promote a 'homely environment and believe that it is important for the children to see where their food is being prepared and appreciate the lovely smells which permeate the building'.

Menu planning

The menus were determined by the two directors and the nursery manager in consultation with the nursery's cooks. Their decisions were based on their existing knowledge on what constitutes a balanced diet, what can be produced in the kitchen and what children are most likely to eat. They also referred to a number of books with specific recipes and advice for feeding under fives. All of the meals are designed to incorporate vegetables. So, for example, carrots may be chopped up finely and incorporated in a lasagne. This works well for Charlton and they are confident that this strategy ensures that the majority of children eat their 'five a day'. A number of foods are specifically excluded from the menu. These are foods which are either unhealthy, microbiologically unsafe or children may be allergic to. These include raw eggs, nuts, honey, processed meats and other foods. They take great care to ensure that sugar and salt levels are kept to a minimum. The menu is designed to rotate over a four-week cycle so that different foods can be provided on different days.

Special dietary requests

Vegetarian, vegan and any other dietary requests can be accommodated. All this information is provided to the kitchen on a daily basis.

Food choice

Food choice is limited and children are served a range of food on their plates. They are encouraged to eat the full range of food available and staff are sensitive to likes and dislikes. Children are not forced to eat foods that they find unacceptable and dessert would always be offered even if a child had not eaten their main course, although staff members always actively encourage children to try new foods.

Parents' influence on food choice

All menus and recipes are displayed in the nursery and provided to parents on request. Parents are invited to give feedback via frequent questionnaires and this is acted on where appropriate. For example, recent feedback from parents resulted in a change from a two-week to a four-week rotating menu. Staff keep brief notes during mealtimes to inform parents how their children have eaten. Staff in the baby room keep detailed notes on quantities consumed, particularly milk taken.

Scheduling

The children at Charlton are offered four meals a day, depending on the length of their day.

- Breakfast of cereal and milk from 8.00 am
- A snack at 10.00 am which comprises a selection of prepared fresh fruit and either organic milk or water
- Two-course lunch at 12.00 noon with water to drink

- Tea at 4.00 pm comprising a savoury sandwich made with homemade bread, organic yoghurt, homemade cake, fruit if requested and either water or organic milk to drink

Juice is generally not given unless it is the only thing a child will drink and upon special request by a parent/carer.

Children who arrive between 8.00 and 8.30 am eat breakfast. The activity preceding all snacks and meals is usually a story. They are then encouraged to use the toilet and wash their hands. Activities after meals vary depending on the time of day. After the morning snack and tea the children are allowed a period of free play. After the main meal, children play outside.

Breakfast and morning snack usually last about 20 minutes, tea 30 minutes and lunch up to 45 minutes. There is no formal policy about meal length. Children are encouraged to be sociable and particularly slow eaters would be given ample opportunity to finish. Water is freely available and children are encouraged to drink more on hot days and when they have been doing energetic activity. Charlton has excellent outdoor space and children are encouraged to play outside as much as possible. This is usually at least twice a day.

Environment

Children eat their meals and snacks on small chairs and tables arranged in sociable groups. The staff are encouraged to eat with the children particularly in the pre-school room, however scheduling staff breaks and assisting smaller children with eating means that this is not always possible in other parts of the Nursery. A range of utensils are available which are suitable for the ages and ability of the children. All children over two use porcelain crockery and knives, forks and spoons. Good manners are encouraged. For example all children are asked to wait until every one is served before they start eating and they must wait until everyone has finished before they use flannels to clean their hands and faces and are allowed to play.

Behavioural issues

Charlton adopts a positive reinforcement policy to all behavioural issues. If a particular undesired behaviour cannot be discouraged using this method, then appropriate supervised time-out may be used.

Children who are fussy eaters and have phobias about food are encouraged to try different types of food. For example, one child who will only eat one food type is given it and other foods are introduced alongside it. Playing with food is acceptable behaviour in the younger children but discouraged as they get older.

Charlton had no experience of older children throwing food or stealing food from others, but if this type of behaviour did occur they would deal with it by explaining the consequences of the particular behaviour to the child. In extreme cases supervised time-out would be used for persistent undesirable behaviour.

Food and play

The children at Charlton are encouraged to participate in cooking activities. This extends to beyond merely assembling food and they have just got permission to allow children into the kitchen to see food being put into the oven. They are also encouraged to role-play with food in home corners and shopping activities.

Food and the curriculum

Charlton meets the early learning goals of the National Curriculum. Children learn about healthy food and balanced diets as part of being healthy. The provision of healthy food and lots of physical activity is part of the ethos of Charlton. The nursery believes the provision of nutritious food and plenty of exercise together with excellent provision for a proper sleep results in healthy children with healthy appetites.

Sample menu

MONDAY

Tuna pasta bake
Fruit and yoghurt

TUESDAY

Hot pot
Fruit and custard

WEDNESDAY

Chicken casserole
Syrup tart and vanilla sauce

THURSDAY

Lamb curry and rice
Fruit salad

FRIDAY

Sausage crunchies and organic baked beans
Semolina

- Breakfast comprises cereal and milk.
- Morning snack: a selection of fresh fruit and milk or water to drink.
- Afternoon tea: savoury sandwiches, cake, organic yoghurt, fresh fruit and water or milk to drink.
- Water is offered as a drink with the main lunchtime meal.
- Vegetarian options are available where requested.

Note: all these main dishes incorporate a significant proportion of vegetables as part of the recipe. They are either puréed into sauces or chopped up finely and incorporated into the main dish.

Case Study 3: First Steps Centre for Children and Families

Profile

First Steps Centre for Children and Families is a registered charity which seeks to respond to the specific needs of local families. There are two distinct areas of work within the centre, the family services and the childcare and education. There are designated staff who work within each of these areas. There is close co-operation and planning between all staff. First Steps nursery has been recognised by the government for its work with families and children with special educational needs, has Early Excellent Centre Status and is an early designated Sure Start Children's Centre. It provides full- and part-time childcare and education to children from the local community with ages ranging from six months to five years. A few children attend for a full day, but the majority attend for a three-hour session during the core hours between 8 am and 6.00 pm. First Steps provides three meals a day, a morning snack, lunch and tea. Children who arrive at 8.00 am often bring their own breakfast or would be offered a choice of cereals.

Preparation

All snacks and meals are prepared by a designated cook, in a purpose built kitchen. The majority of the ingredients are sourced locally. Meat comes from a local butcher as the nursery is keen to ensure that quality products are used. Fruit and vegetables are delivered by Sainsburys and other groceries come from a cash and carry. Organic foods are not routinely used in meal preparation and the nursery manager cited cost as the major influence on this decision. She added that without these constraints they would probably opt for organic alternatives where practicable. The kitchen itself is at the centre of the nursery and children are aware that their food is prepared there.

Menu planning

The head of centre, head of nursery and cook all contribute to the menus. Menus are based on good nutritional practice, what the children are likely to eat and the availability of seasonal items such as vegetables. No particular publication was relied on to inform this process and the nursery manager was confident that her knowledge of food and nutrition together with the cook's previous experience of working in a residential care home resulted in a balanced and varied menu. A number of foods are specifically excluded from the menu: raw eggs, nuts, honey, processed meats. No salt is added to foods and where processed food is used salt levels are checked on labels. The menu is designed to rotate over a five-week cycle and ensures that within this different foods are provided on different days.

Special dietary requests

Vegetarian options are available. Any other special requests are discussed with parents prior to enrolment. The nursery manager did add that there were only a small number of children from ethnic minority backgrounds and that if that situation changed, they would take a more proactive approach to specific cultural and religious requirements.

Food choice

At morning snack the children can choose from a range of foods on offer. This would typically include fruit, cheese, breadsticks, and so on, with milk or water to drink. They would be encouraged to take one piece of fruit and other food type on offer. At lunchtime the food is placed on the table in serving dishes. There is a rule that children should have a small portion of everything on offer on their plate and they are encouraged to try everything. However, they would not be forced to eat anything that they did not want to. Stickers are given as a reward for children who try all the food on their plate. Desserts are not offered as rewards for clean plates.

Parents' influence on food choice

The parents of children at First Steps have no real input into the menu. However positive comments were received on appointment of the current cook who makes great efforts to use fresh ingredients where possible. Menus are displayed and are available to parents. Where there are any concerns about the quantity and variety of foods that a particular child is eating, this is recorded in a food diary and reported to parents on a daily basis.

Scheduling

- First Steps provides three meals a day.
- A snack at about 10.30 am which typically comprises a selection of fruit, or rice cakes, or crudités and a drink of milk and water.
- Two course lunch at 12.30 pm with water to drink.
- Tea at 4.00 pm comprises savouries such as sandwiches, pizza and yoghurt or cake and a drink of milk and water (for a typical menu see page 76).

Immediately before all snacks and meals, children help to tidy up their last activity and then use the toilet and wash their hands. In the morning the snack is preceded by group time and in the afternoon by a programmed activity. Lunch is preceded by group singing activity and followed by play in the garden. First Steps take every opportunity to make as much use of their outdoor space as possible and many activities are scheduled, weather permitting, in the garden. Snack time usually lasts about 20 minutes and lunch and tea about 30. There is no formal policy about meal length and there is an emphasis on eating as a social event. Individual requests for additional or different food and drink are assessed on a case-by-case basis. The nursery manager cited the cases of children who refuse to drink anything else but juice. Practice at First Steps would allow this in the first instance but gradually dilute the juice in the feeding cups until such a time that the child was happy to accept water.

Environment

Children eat their meals and snacks at tables in their main play area. They eat in self-selected friendship groups of up to six children and are supervised on a table basis with an adult who eats with the children. The children do not help with the table setting but are allocated preferred chores, such as collecting cups and plates as a reward for good behaviour.

Utensils

A range of utensils is available, suitable for the ages and ability of the children. They are encouraged to eat using utensils but not to the exclusion of eating their food. If children have any particular special needs they are discussed with the parents and can be accommodated.

Behavioural issues

First Steps adopts a positive reinforcement policy to all behavioural issues. Children who are finicky eaters and phobic about food, would be encouraged to try the variety of foods on offer. Playing with food is tolerated among the younger children but discouraged as they get older. Slow eaters would be allowed plenty of time to finish their food but the others would be allowed to leave the table. Other unacceptable behaviour would be discouraged by ignoring and praising those children who are modelling good behaviour. In extreme cases, consequences of the behaviour would be discussed and then followed by supervised time-out.

Food and play

The children are encouraged to participate in cooking activities. There is a separate area designated for these 'investigative' activities. This is well equipped with microwave oven, and two-ring electric burner. The staff also have access to an oven in the family room. Children make a range of foods for example fruit kebabs, pizzas, cakes, cheese straws. The nursery manager commented that she thought it was important that children made a range of foods and not just the less healthy cakes and biscuits which feature in many children's cooking sessions.

They are also developing their own vegetable garden, where vegetables which are grown in the garden are then used by the cook for the children's food. This has been a great success and even reluctant vegetable eaters are keen to eat their own produce. Role-play is encouraged and there is a home corner for cooking and various shops and stalls and restaurants.

Food and the curriculum

First Steps meets the early learning goals of the National Curriculum and children learn about healthy food and balanced diets as part of being healthy.

Other issues

The manager also commented that staff participate in continuing professional development activities and that two members had recently attended an infant and toddler forum study day accredited by the Royal College of Nursing and British Dietitians Association on feeding infants and toddlers. This focused on behavioural issues and reinforced their existing policy and practice.

The nursery is part of the family centre where various activities take place designed to help children and their families. Recent activities included 'sticky fingers' a cooking activity for the under fives and a course run by the local food co-op which focused on cooking for parents.

Sample menu

MONDAY

Break	Fresh fruit
Lunch	Chicken stew and dumplings with potatoes
	Arctic roll
Tea	Scotch eggs, salad and jam tarts

TUESDAY

Break	Fresh fruit
Lunch	Jacket potatoes with tuna mayonnaise and coleslaw or cheese and beans
	Ice cream and sauce
Tea	Crumpets and cakes

WEDNESDAY

Break	Rice cakes
Lunch	Savoury mince, potato wedges, cauliflower
	Carrots and peas
	Fruit and cream
Tea	Sandwich selection and fromage frais

THURSDAY

Break	Fresh fruit
Lunch	Beef curry and rice
	Fruit fool and cream
Tea	Crackers and cheese and fromage frais

FRIDAY

Break	Fresh fruit
Lunch	Sausages, mashed potatoes, with vegetables and onion gravy
	Rice pudding
Tea	Beans on toast and fruit trifle

Children are offered milk or water to drink with all meals and snacks.
Vegetarian alternatives are available where required.

Case Study 4: childminders

Profile

Rachel is a registered childminder and provides childcare for up to three children under five. She currently looks after three children aged between 18 months and three years of age. She knows all of the parents well and to date she has an existing friendship with most of them. Rachel is in sole charge of the children and prepares and supervises all the meals and snacks. The setting is typical of a home environment with a kitchen and large sitting room where there is plenty of child friendly space for the children to play.

Rachel provides three meals a day. Most children have their breakfast before they arrive, however sometimes the children will have extra cereal or a piece of toast as they often arrive when Rachel's own children are having their breakfast.

Preparation

All the food is prepared by Rachel. She mostly plans her shopping on a weekly basis and buys most of the food from the local supermarket. She does not stick to a published menu but tries to ensure that children eat a nutritious and balanced diet. She does not rely on any specific publications or books but did say that when she attended her childminder's course that some time was spent on healthy eating and food hygiene. Rachel is a trained teacher and has good knowledge of the components of a balanced diet. She mentioned the importance of 'five a day' and appropriate amounts of protein and carbohydrate.

Menu planning

Menu planning is done on a daily basis, although a certain amount of advance planning does occur as this influences what she buys in the weekly shop. She specifically excludes certain foods from meals. These include lightly cooked eggs, nuts, burgers. She avoids using too much salt and has a preference for white meat over red.

Special dietary requests

Special dietary requests are dealt with on an individual basis. One of the advantages of childcare in a home setting is that particular likes, dislikes and phobias can be dealt with very effectively. Rachel always discusses any particular feeding issues with parents and they agree a strategy appropriate to the individual child and circumstances.

Food choice

Food choice is limited. However, at lunchtime, the children have some choice and the older children often help with the preparation of sandwiches, and so on. Rachel believes that she has the flexibility to be sensitive to likes and dislikes. Children are encouraged to eat a range of foods available and explore new tastes and textures. They are not forced to eat foods that they find unacceptable and dessert is not used as a reward for a clean plate.

Parents' influence on food choice

The parents have a limited input into the menu. When she first meets a prospective parent she shows them her 'childminding information file' which contains a list of things that she tends to cook and gives examples of typical meals. Rachel added that as most of the parents are friends, they are aware of the sort of food she is likely to prepare and seem happy with what is on offer. She would always discuss any particular feeding issues with parents and would ask permission to allow children to have the odd treat such as an ice cream or chocolate.

Scheduling

The children are offered four meals or snacks a day.

- A snack at 10.30 am would typically comprise cereal and raisins or a piece of fruit with milk, water or fruit squash to drink.
- Lunch consisting of savoury sandwiches, cucumber, tomatoes, celery, raw carrot and yoghurt or fruit with milk, water or squash to drink.
- Snack at 3.30 pm when her other children come in from school often consists of a cereal bar with milk, water or squash to drink.
- A two course main meal at 5.00 pm which always includes some form of carbohydrate such as pasta, potatoes or rice, some form of protein and vegetables. Dessert is always fruit or yoghurt.

Inevitably the daily schedule is less formal than in some nursery settings and activities preceding and following meals vary depending on what Rachel has planned, what the children want to do and in some instances what the weather permits.

Environment

Typically children would tidy up toys before a meal or snack and then sit down in either the sitting room or at the kitchen table. Rachel always sits with the children and often eats with them. The children are encouraged to help with simple chores, for example the older children help prepare the lunch, help clear away and a current favourite activity with one child is to do the washing up.

Utensils

A variety of utensils is provided which are suitable for the ages and ability of the children. Children are encouraged to use utensils properly but not to the exclusion of eating their food.

Behavioural issues

Rachel adopts a positive reinforcement policy to all behavioural issues. Unacceptable behaviour is mostly ignored and good behaviour praised. In cases where unacceptable behaviour is affecting others, or is persistent, then supervised time-out would be considered.

Fussy and finicky eaters are encouraged to choose from a variety of foods. Playing with food is tolerated when children are younger but discouraged as they get older. Slow eaters would be allowed to continue at their own pace but food would be removed if it was clear that they were no longer hungry or interested.

Food and play

The children participate in a range of activities. They have a home corner and regularly play at shopping and preparing food. They use real food to explore textures and participate in 'mixing' activities. They also take part in cooking activities, and often help to make the lunch and make cakes and biscuits.

Food and the curriculum

Rachel is a teacher and is familiar with the early learning goals. She does not however have to adhere to them as part of her registration. She is confident that children learn about healthy foods, through eating balanced meals, play and discussion at meal times.

Sample three day menu*

MONDAY

Break	Fresh fruit
Lunch	Tuna in pitta bread, cucumber, tomatoes, carrot sticks
	Apple/raisins.
Tea	Cottage pie, sweetcorn, peas
	Fruit/yoghurt

THURSDAY

Lunch	Cheese on toast, cucumber, tomatoes, celery
	Banana/grapes
Tea	Roast chicken, boiled potatoes, carrots, swede
	Fruit/yoghurt

FRIDAY

Lunch	Ham/cheese/chicken sandwich, cucumber, tomatoes, carrot sticks/pepper slices
	Peach/pear slices
Tea	Tuna pasta bake, carrots, peas
	Fruit/yoghurt

Morning snack typically comprises dried fruit or a rice cake and a drink of milk, juice or water.
Water or juice is offered with lunch and tea.
* The childminder only cares for children on three days.

Sample Menus Source: The Caroline Walker Trust. Eating well for under 5's in childcare 1998

Menu 1 is a sample menu for a one-week period. The food and drinks in this menu provide the recommended amounts of energy and nutrients for children in childcare for a full day. Children in half-day care including lunch would get the recommended amounts by having the mid-morning snacks and lunches shown on the menu. Children in half-day care including tea would get the recommended amounts by having the mid-afternoon snacks and teas.

Menus 1 and 2 meet the nutritional guidelines for an average 3 year old in child care for a full day. A 4–5 year old will require, and want, larger portions at meals and snacks as will children who do not drink milk. Water should always be available as a drink

Menu 1: an example menu for a child in full day care

	Monday	Tuesday	Wednesday	Thursday	Friday
Example breakfast	Orange juice 25 ml (diluted with water), cornflakes 15 g, milk 50 ml, brown toast 15 g, margarine 3 g, honey/jam 5 g. Breakfast is encouraged either at home or in childcare. This is not included in the nutritional analysis				
Mid-morning snack e.g. at 10.00 am	Milk 100 ml Muffin 40 g Margarine 4 g	Milk 100 ml Crumpet 40 g Margarine 4 g	Milk 100 ml Teacake 30 g Margarine 4 g	Milk 100 ml Oatcakes 26 g Margarine 4 g	Milk 100 ml Scone 30 g Margarine 4 g
Lunch e.g. at 12.00–1.00 pm	Chicken and vegetable curry 100 g Rice 80 g Blackcurrant crumble 80 g	Shepherd's pie 150 g Peas 30 g Stewed apple and dates 60 g Custard 60 g	Tuna, bean and sweet corn pasta 140 g Sponge pudding 60 g Custard 60 g	Lamb burger 80 g Carrots 40 g Oven chips 50 g Rice pudding with sultanas 100 g	Fish fingers 60 g Potatoes 60 g Broccoli 40 g Milk jelly 100 g
Mid-afternoon snack e.g. at 3.00 pm	Milk 100 ml Carrot sticks 30 g Brown bread 25 g Margarine 7g Egg 25 g	Milk 100 ml Apple 50 g Breadsticks 20 g Cheese 25 g	Milk 100 ml Banana 50 g Plain popcorn 20 g	Milk 100 ml Brown toast 25 g Margarine 7 g Marmite 2 g Raisins 20 g	Milk 100 ml Flapjack 30 g Grapes 30 g
Tea e.g. at 5.00 pm	Orange juice 25 ml diluted with water Baked beans 80 g Brown toast 25 g Margarine 7 g Apple 50 g Fromage frais 60 g	Orange juice 25 ml diluted with water Cheese 30 g Brown toast 25 g Margarine 7 g Celery 20 g Fruit salad 60 g	Orange juice 25 ml diluted with water Scone 30 g Margarine 4 g Ham 20 g Cucumber 20 g Tinned pineapple 50 g	Orange juice 25 ml diluted with water Pizza 60 g Tomato 40 g Apple 50 g Fruit yoghurt 60 g	Orange juice 25 ml diluted with water Pasta 60 g Tomato sauce 40 g Cheese 20 g Mandarin orange 50 g

Menu 2

This menu includes examples of meals, snacks and drinks which are suitable for vegetarian children and for particular ethnic groups. Individual menu planners will need to use their skill to provide meals that are acceptable to the particular group of children or individuals in their care.

	Monday	Tuesday	Wednesday	Thursday	Friday
Example breakfast	Orange juice 25 ml (diluted with water), cornflakes 15 g, milk 50 ml, brown toast 15 g, margarine 3 g, honey/jam 5 g. Breakfast is encouraged either at home or in childcare. This is not included in the nutritional analysis				
Mid-morning snack e.g. at 10.00 am	Milk 100 ml Muffin 40 g Margarine 4 g	Milk 100 ml Crumpet 40 g Margarine 4 g	Milk 100 ml Teacake 30 g Margarine 4 g	Milk 100 ml Oatcakes 26 g Margarine 4 g	Milk 100 ml Scone 30 g Margarine 4 g
Lunch e.g. at 12.00–1.00 pm	Wholemeal cheese and egg quiche 100 g Baked beans 80 g Banana 50 g	Fried tofu 60 g Stir fried vegetables 80 g Noodles 60 g Milk/soya fruit yoghurt 60 g	Potato curry 60 g Rice 80 g Dahl 50 g Chapatti 20 g Orange 80 g	Pasta 80 g Tomato sauce 40 g Cheese 20 g Broccoli 40 g Dried fruit salad 100 g	Baked sweet potato 80 g Rice and peas 80 g Spinach 30 g Pineapple 80 g
Mid-afternoon snack e.g. at 3.00 pm	Milk 100 ml Carrot sticks 30 g Brown bread 25 g Margarine 7 g Egg 25 g	Milk 100 ml Apple 50 g Breadsticks 20 g Cheese 25 g	Milk 100 ml Banana 50 g Plain popcorn 20 g	Milk 100 ml Brown toast 25 g Margarine 7 g Marmite 2 g Raisins 20 g	Milk 100 ml Flapjack 30 g Grapes 30 g
Tea e.g. at 5.00 pm	Orange juice 25 ml diluted with water Baked beans 80 g Brown toast 25 g Margarine 7 g Apple 50 g Fromage frais 60 g	Orange juice 25 ml diluted with water Scrambled egg 60 g Brown toast 25 g Margarine 7 g Celery 20 g Fruit salad 60 g	Orange juice 25 ml diluted with water Scone 30 g Margarine 4 g Hummus 15 g Cucumber 20 g Egg custard tart 60 g	Orange juice 25 ml diluted with water Pizza 60 g Tomato 40 g Apple 50 g Fruit yoghurt 60 g	Orange juice 25 ml diluted with water Pasta 60 g Cheese sauce 40 g Sweet corn 30 g Mandarin orange 50 g

- Successful feeding strategies depend on diet, appetite, the ability of the child to eat and the eating environment.

- Menus should be balanced, healthy and incorporate foods from the four main food groups.

- It is important to recognise food is inextricably linked with children's family life and culture. Cultural and religious beliefs which may affect food acceptability should be discussed with parents and guardians.

- Children should be exposed to a variety of foods and given the opportunity to experience different textures and flavours.

- Appetite is influenced by mealtimes and levels of physical activity. Food should be seen in the context of an overall approach to encouraging healthy lifestyles.

- Careful consideration should be given to the eating environment and the implements that children use to eat their food. It is widely accepted that mealtimes should be sociable occasions where adults as far as possible eat with children.

- Discipline at mealtimes should be managed as part of an overall behaviour management strategy. Most effective results appear to be obtained with positive reinforcement strategies combined with supervised time out for extreme examples of bad behaviour.

- Children's understanding of food is best achieved by embedding it in the curriculum.

Find out more

- Books such as *Feeding your Child for Lifelong Health* by Roberts, Hayman and Tracy give a good insight into physical, medical and psychological factors which may affect feeding in young children.

- *Eating Well for Under fives in Childcare* produced by the Caroline Walker Trust gives practical and nutritional guidelines relevant to childcare settings.

- Martin Herbert discusses these issues in more detail in *Coping with Children's Feeding Problems and Bedtime Battles* produced by the British Psychological Society.

Food safety and hygiene

The importance of food safety

Food safety is essential to healthy diets. Many of the nurseries and schools that you will work for will provide food for the children in their care. This can range from the preparation of small simple snacks to full menus including breakfast, lunch and dinner. Parents and carers expect that the food eaten by their children is safe and it is not unreasonable for them to expect those who are involved in the preparation to have done everything possible to keep it safe.

Incidences of food poisoning

Over recent years the number of reported cases of food-borne illness has dropped. There are however still more than 70,000 cases of food poisoning each year in the UK and it is widely accepted that the true number of cases is likely to be much higher. Think of 70,000 as the tip of an iceberg shown in Figure 6.1. Most of the official figures are reported by doctors who see patients with symptoms of food poisoning. Many people may suffer the symptoms of food poisoning but do not bother going to their doctor. These cases account for the remaining 9 million people thought to be affected each year.

Table 6.1 Food poisoning notifications – annual totals England and Wales 1982–2004

Year	Total	Formally notified	Otherwise ascertained
1982	14,253	9,964	4,289
1983	17,735	12,273	5,462
1984	20,702	13,247	7,455
1985	19,242	13,143	6,099
1986	23,948	16,502	7,446
1987	29,331	20,363	8,968
1988	39,713	27,826	11,887
1989	52,557	38,086	14,471
1990	52,145	36,945	15,200
1991	52,543	35,291	17,252
1992	63,347	42,551	20,796
1993	68,587	44,271	24,316
1994	81,833	50,412	31,421
1995	82,041	50,761	31,280
1996	83,233	50,718	32,515
1997	93,901	54,233	39,668
1998	93,932	53,764	40,168
1999	86,316	48,454	37,862
2000	86,528	46,481	40,047
2001	85,468	46,768	38,700
2002	72,649	38,541	34,108
2003	70,895	35,695	35,200
2004	70,311	34,376	35,935

Source: Statutory Notifications of Infectious Diseases (NOIDs)

Food safety and the law

All childcare settings providing food will be registered with the Environmental Health Department in the local authority in which they are situated. Environmental Health Practitioners (EHPs) will inspect them from time to time to ensure that they comply with current food hygiene regulations.

Owners and managers have a specific responsibility to provide essential food safety facilities such as a suitably equipped kitchen and hand washing facilities. It is also their responsibility to ensure that they operate a food safety management system based on the principles of Hazard Analysis Critical Control Point (HACCP) and that anyone involved in the preparation of handling of food is suitably trained.

If you deal with food as part of your job, then you will be classed as a food handler and have a legal responsibility to keep food safe. Your level of responsibility will depend on your position within the organisation which you work. The law requires that you are trained commensurate with your work activity. This would normally be

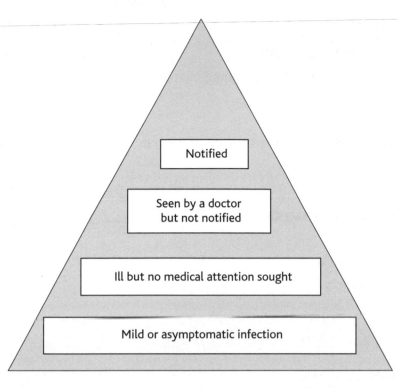

Source: Wall 1996. Food poisoning: notifications, laboratory reports and outbreaks – where do the statistics come from and what do they mean. *Communicable Disease Review*. 6, 93–100.

Figure 6.1 Steps from infection to notification

determined by your employer. Detailed information on the knowledge that is appropriate for your level of responsibility can be found in Chartered Institute of Environmental Health Publications which accompany their food hygiene qualifications.

Food hazards

Food hazards are anything that could cause harm or injury to children or adults who might consume the food. Small children may be particularly vulnerable to food hazards such as food poisoning bacteria as their immune systems are not fully developed. A small proportion of adults and children may also be allergic to food or ingredients, for example peanuts, which may be perfectly safe for a normal person to eat but may cause a severe allergic reaction if eaten by them. Food hazards include:

- Biological hazards such as salmonella
- Physical hazards such as bits of glass
- Chemical hazards such as cleaning fluids

As you can see from the list below food hazards are numerous and have the potential to affect food at any point in the food chain that exists between the farm on which the raw materials are produced and the fork of the consumer who eats the food. It is important to remember that hazards are a possible danger. They only become an actual danger when they contaminate food. Food hygiene is about not letting that happen.

Types of hazard

Examples of biological hazards

- Bacteria that can cause food poisoning or spoilage
- Viruses
- Fungi
- Naturally occurring poisons which are sometimes found in plants, fish and fungi
- Parasites

Examples of physical hazards

- Broken glass
- Packaging materials
- Parts of machinery
- Dirt
- Jewellery
- Hair
- Fingernails
- Bodies of pests

Examples of chemical hazards

- Pesticides used in food production
- Cleaning chemicals
- Dissolved metals

Biological hazards

Biological hazards are the main cause of food-borne diseases with most cases being caused by bacteria. Other causes include viruses, parasites and poisonous plants, fish and fungi.

Bacteria

Bacteria are single celled micro-organisms which are too small to see without a microscope. They exist all around us and are vital to our existence. A small proportion of bacteria are described as pathogenic and can be harmful.

Sources of pathogenic bacteria

The bacteria that can cause food poisoning come from a variety of sources including:

- Raw food such as vegetables and raw meat may be a source of pathogenic bacteria. Vegetables are often covered in soil and animal products such as meat can be contaminated from bacteria which were present in the intestine of the animal.

- Water: untreated or contaminated water may carry pathogenic bacteria. It is important that all water used in food premises is correctly treated and protected from contamination.

- People are a prime source of bacteria. They can be found on skin, hair, ears nose, throat and in cuts and pimples. Poor personal hygiene such as not washing hands after using the toilet may also result in food being contaminated.

- Air, dirt, dust may all be sources of bacteria. The air carries millions of microscopic particles that may all be contaminated by bacteria. This is one reason why it is important to ensure that food is always kept covered.

- Food waste: waste produced when preparing food is also problematic. It is likely to be contaminated, may not be cooked and must be kept separate from food which is going to be eaten. It may also attract pests that may also contaminate food and should therefore be stored and disposed of properly.

- Pests and pets: these include insects such as flies and cockroaches and animals such as rats, mice, birds, cats and dogs or indeed any household pet. They all carry harmful bacteria on their bodies and in their faeces.

Other biological hazards

These include viruses, parasites and poisonous plants, fungi and fish.

- Viruses: these are carried on food and in water. One of the main sources is sewage and contaminated water. They have the potential to contaminate any type of food. However they are mainly associated with water, shellfish and raw food such as salad and raw vegetables.

- Parasites: these live in or on other organisms. The parasites that cause illness associated with food include roundworms, flatworms and flukes that live in raw meat and fish.

- Naturally poisonous foods: these include red kidney beans which have not been boiled enough, rhubarb leaves, certain type of fungi and parts of fish such as the Japanese fugu fish.

Physical hazards

Physical hazards are often a source of consumer complaint. Finding a hair or a cigarette end in a meal is an unpleasant experience. In some instances physical contamination may cause more serious harm such as a cut mouth, broken tooth or choking. This is a particular concern in very young children who may find it difficult to distinguish between the food they are eating and a foreign body present in it.

It is inevitable that physical contaminants from various stages in the food chain may find their way into food. Be assured that most manufacturers go to extreme lengths during production to ensure that this does not happen. Your role is to be vigilant and examine raw materials before use, wash and sieve ingredients as appropriate and ensure that packaging does not contaminate food.

It is more likely that physical contamination in the nursery environment will come from personal items such as hair, fingernails, jewellery, clothing, plasters or packaging. This can be avoided by ensuring that good standards of personal hygiene are maintained and dress codes adhered to.

Chemical hazards

Chemical hazards normally occur as a result of the accidental addition of a chemical to food. These can include:

- Lubricants and cleaning chemicals used in the work place
- Chemical contaminants in the environment which may contaminate raw materials
- Agricultural or veterinary residues used in primary production
- Misuse of additives such as food colours or preservatives

The symptoms of chemical food poisoning may occur fairly quickly and be similar to those of food poisoning (vomiting, diarrhoea, abdominal pain) or manifest themselves months or even years later for example where people eat a small amount of a chemical over a long period.

Food illness

When people eat or drink contaminated food, they can become ill. There are three types of illness linked to food:

- Food poisoning is caused by pathogenic bacteria that are living on the food or harmful substances such as poisonous plants, fish or fungi, chemicals, metals or toxins.
- Food-borne disease is caused by consuming food or water which is carrying the harmful bacteria or viruses.
- Food allergies affect a small yet significant proportion of the population who become ill after eating a product such as nuts that are not normally harmful to others.

Most food-borne illness is caused by eating food that is contaminated by pathogenic bacteria.

Food poisoning

Pathogenic bacteria cause most food poisoning. Examples include:

- *Salmonella* spp
- *Staphylococcus aureus*
- *Clostridium perfringens*
- *Clostridium botulinum*
- *Bacillus cereus*

People feel ill when the body detects that they have eaten something harmful and responds by trying to eject the food. Hence the most common symptoms of:

- Nausea
- Vomiting
- Diarrhoea
- Abdominal pain

This normally occurs, depending on which bacterium has caused the illness, between eight and 36 hours after eating the food. However there are some bacteria such as *Bacillus cereus* which produce toxins in the food before it is eaten which can make people feel sick in as little as one hour. Most food poisoning lasts for 24 to 48 hours. However in some people it can continue for a week or more and can be life threatening. Young children, the elderly and sick can be particularly vulnerable.

Food-borne disease

Food-borne diseases are caused by micro-organisms that are carried by food or water. Only a small number of these micro-organisms is necessary to cause disease. Examples include:

- Bacteria such as *Campylobacter jejuni, Escherichia coli 0157, Listeria monocytogenes*
- Viruses such as Norovirus
- Parasites such as tapeworms

The effects of the illness are similar to those of food poisoning. The symptoms normally take longer to appear – days, weeks or months – and the illness can last for a day or continue for many years and present serious long-term health problems.

Food allergies

These can cause particular concern in nurseries as very young children will not be aware that they are allergic to certain foods and will not know what to avoid. It is important that the ingredients of food served in nurseries are checked to ensure that there are no foods that children may be allergic to and those on restricted diets stick to them. Food allergies are a type of food intolerance where the immune response reacts as if the body is under attack. Allergic reactions often occur within minutes of eating the sensitive food or may take several hours. Reactions may be mild, but in extreme cases may result in death. Symptoms may include:

- Sickness
- Diarrhoea
- Abdominal cramps
- Rashes
- Tingling of lips, tongue and throat
- Swelling of the throat
- Difficulty in breathing and speaking

Anaphylactic shock

This is a type of allergy which is life threatening. The symptoms start with a mild reaction but can develop into swelling, difficulty in breathing, a drop in blood pressure, collapse and unconsciousness.

Table 6.2 Examples of food poisoning

Bacterium	Incubation period	Symptoms	Reservoir	Transmission
Salmonella spp	12–72 hours	Diarrhoea Vomiting Fever	Wild and domestic animals and birds and occasionally humans	Red and white meats, raw eggs milk and dairy products, following contamination of cooked foods by raw food or failing to achieve adequate cooking temperatures. Person-to-person spread by close contact. Contact with infected animals.
Staphylococcus aureus	1–7 hours (usually 2–4 hours)	Vomiting, abdominal pain	Infected exposed skin lesions, nostrils or fingers of food handlers. Rarely infected animals.	Handling cooked foods such as ham, meat, poultry, fish, prawns and cream cakes which are then stored at room temperature for more than two hours and eaten cold. Some outbreaks are associated with canned foods contaminated after processing.
Bacillus cereus	1–5 hours or 8 to 16 hours depending on type of food poisoning	Either nausea and vomiting or abdominal pain or diarrhoea depending on type of food poisoning	Environment, for example soil, sediments, dust vegetation. Food such as cereal products, herbs and spices, dried foods, milk and dairy products, meat and meat products.	Contaminated cooked foods subjected to inadequate post-cooking temperature control during cooling and storage. Mainly affects rice dishes, occasionally pasta, meat or vegetable dishes, dairy products, soups, sauces, sweet pastry products
Clostridium perfringens	8–22 hours (usually 12–18 hours)	Diarrhoea and abdominal pain	Intestines of food animals, soil and dust.	Contaminated meat and poultry dishes subjected to inadequate temperature control after cooking during cooling and storage.

Source: Compiled from information obtained from the Health Protection Agency (HPA)
http://www.hpa.org.uk/infections/topics_az/list.htm

Food poisoning – how does it happen?

Food poisoning is commonly caused by eating food described as high risk. These foods provide the ideal conditions for bacteria to multiply to levels that may cause illness.

Table 6.3 Examples of food borne disease

Bacterium	Incubation period	Symptoms	Reservoir	Transmission
Campylobacter	1 to 11 days usually 2–5 days	Abdominal pain, profuse diarrhoea, malaise. Vomiting is uncommon.	Intestines of birds, particularly poultry and animals, cattle and domestic pets.	Raw or undercooked meat (especially poultry), unpasteurised milk, bird pecked on doorsteps, untreated water, and domestic pets with diarrhoea. Person-to-person if personal hygiene is poor.
E coli 0157	1 to 6 days	Haemorrhagic colitis, haemolytic uraemic syndrome	Intestines of cattle and possibly other domesticated animals	Contaminated foodstuffs – beef and beef products such as undercooked beefburgers. Milk and vegetables have also been associated with outbreaks. Person-to-person spread can occur by direct contact particularly in nurseries and schools. Contact with infected animals on farms.
Listeria	3 to 70 days	Influenza like illness spontaneous abortion	Environment, cattle, sheep, soil, silage. Has also been isolated from a range of raw foods including vegetables and uncooked meats as well as processed foods. A wide range of food products have been implicated in outbreaks including soft cheeses and meat based pâtés.	The majority of cases are believed to be food-borne. Some cases by direct contact with animals. Mother to foetus during pregnancy or via person-to-person spread between infants shortly after birth.

Source: Compiled from information obtained from the Health Protection Agency (HPA)
http://www.hpa.org.uk/infections/topics_az/list.htm

Examples of high risk foods

- Cooked meat and poultry
- Cooked meat products, for example gravy and stews
- Meat or fish pâtés
- Milk, eggs and lightly cooked dishes containing them, for example, mayonnaise and mousses

- Shellfish
- Cooked rice
- Prepared salads and vegetables
- Delicatessen products

The process of multiplication is called binary fission. This takes place every ten to 20 minutes under ideal conditions. It is possible for one bacterium to produce millions of bacteria in a few hours and this may be enough to cause food poisoning.

Ideal conditions for bacterial growth

A combination of conditions is required for bacteria to multiply to numbers that will cause illness. These include:

- Food
- Moisture
- Warmth
- Time

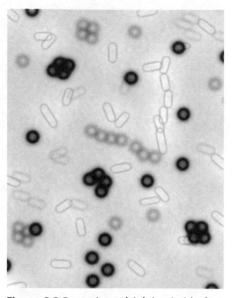

Figure 6.2 Bacteria multiplying in ideal conditions

Food and moisture

Bacteria prefer foods that are moist and high in protein. These are known as high-risk foods.

Time and temperature

Most food poisoning organisms multiply at between 5°C and 63°C. This temperature range is commonly referred to as the danger zone. The ideal temperature for the multiplication is 37°C which is the same as body temperature. At temperatures at less than 5°C most bacteria stop reproducing and keeping food in the refrigerator is one way of preventing food poisoning bacteria from multiplying. Freezing will inactivate bacteria but will not kill them and bacteria on frozen food will continue to reproduce once thawed food enters the danger zone (between 5°C and 63°C).

Cooking at high temperatures for long enough will kill most bacteria. Food needs to be cooked so that internal temperatures reach at least 75°C. Some bacteria, however, can survive by forming spores, which are capable of surviving cooking and other harsh conditions. They do not multiply in this form. However, once conditions are favourable again, they emerge from their spores and continue to multiply.

Most bacteria divide every 20 minutes therefore it is essential that the time that high risk food is present in the danger zone is kept to a minimum.

Time and temperature control

Clearly, avoiding the contamination of food in the first place would be the most effective way of preventing food poisoning. However, we are surrounded by bacteria, and even the most scrupulous cleaning regimes will not prevent bacteria from coming into contact with food. Controlling temperature is one of the most effective ways of preventing bacteria multiplying.

Examples of poor practice that can lead to illness

- Cooling food too slowly before refrigeration
- Leaving food at ambient temperatures
- Inadequate reheating of food
- Undercooking meat and poultry
- Not thawing frozen food sufficiently before cooking
- Keeping hot food at temperatures under 63°C for long enough periods to allow for the multiplication of bacteria

Childcare settings in common with many other premises where food is prepared and eaten have to adhere to strict temperature control regimes that involve three main types of action:

- Restricting the times that high risk food are in the danger zone to less than four hours
- Using low temperatures such as refrigeration and freezing to minimise multiplication of bacteria
- Using high temperatures by cooking food properly

The nature of food preparation means that it is impossible to keep foods out of the danger zone altogether. Food handlers must avoid leaving food in situations that could be in the danger zone.

Measuring temperatures

Measuring temperatures is one way of checking that food is cooked properly and is subsequently not being stored in the temperature danger zone. You will have probably noticed that those who prepare and serve food commonly check the temperatures of refrigerators, freezers and the food itself. If it is your job to check the temperature you should have received training in:

- Checking the temperature
- How to record the temperature
- What to do if the temperature is unsafe
- Cleaning the thermometer before and after use to avoid contaminating food

Table 6.4 Checking temperatures

Stage of food production	Recommended temperatures
Delivery	0°C to 5°C* for refrigerated foods
Storage	
● Refrigerator or cold store	0°C to 5°C*
● Deep freezer	−18°C or below
Thawing	0°C to 5°C* preferably in a refrigerator
Preparation (high risk foods)	Avoid temperature danger zone of 5*–63°C for long periods of time
Cooking	Minimum core temperature of 75°C
Cooling	10°C or cooler (ideally 5°C or cooler) within 90 minutes*
Re-heating	Minimum core temperature of 75°C
Hot holding	Minimum core temperature of 63°C
Cold holding	0°C to 5°C is recommended

*The legal requirement for cold holding is 8°C

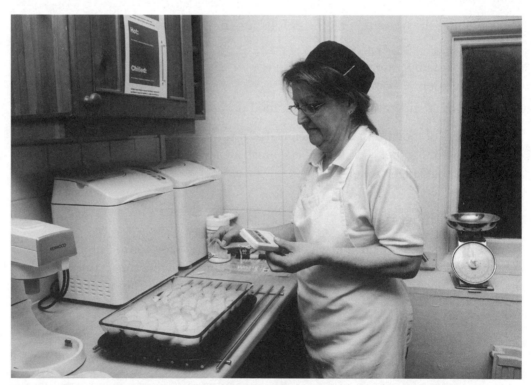

Figure 6.3 Using a probe thermometer to check the temperature of cooked food

Personal hygiene

Most of you will understand the importance of making sure that you are clean and tidy. This sets a good example to the children in your care and creates a good impression with their parents. Good standards of personal hygiene when handling food go beyond creating a good impression, as human beings can be, and commonly

Figure 6.4 Wearing appropriate protective clothing

are a source of food poisoning bacteria and various physical and chemical contaminants.

Keeping hands clean

It is absolutely essential that all nursery workers maintain good standards of hand hygiene through frequent and effective washing and drying. Even healthy people may have bacteria living on their bodies which may transfer from hands and onto foods. *Staphylococcus aureus* is an example of a bacterium which is found on the skin of humans.

Effective hand washing:

● Removes bacteria, viruses and dirt from hands

● Prevents direct and cross contamination of food by hands

When to wash your hands

Before

● Starting work

● Touching high risk food

During

● Any work with food

● Whenever hands are soiled

● When switching between raw and high risk food

After

- Visiting the toilet
- Changing nappies
- Handling sick children
- Handling raw foods
- Coughing, sneezing or touching handkerchiefs
- Touching face or hair
- After cleaning or touching any chemicals
- Handling pets
- Handling rubbish or touching waste bins
- After eating, drinking or smoking

Wash hands in warm soapy water.

Dry hands thoroughly.

Figure 6.5 How to wash your hands
© Food and Drink Federation (foodlink – www.foodlink.org.uk). Reproduced with permission.

How to wash your hands

1 Always use a designated wash hand basin.

2 Use soap and warm water. The warmth of the water helps loosen grease on your hands which traps bacteria.

3 Rub the soap over both sides of your hands. It is important not to miss any areas.

4 Rub the soap between every finger and around the thumbnails. People often miss between their fingers and around their nails.

5 Rinse off with clean, warm water.

6 Dry hands thoroughly. More bacteria spread from damp hands than dry hands. Use a paper towel or hand dryer.

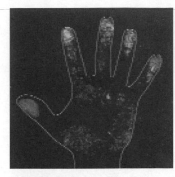

Bacteria on hand after using the toilet.

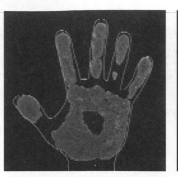

Bacteria on hand after touching old dishcloth.

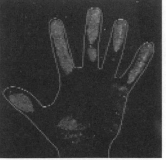

Bacteria on hand after handling raw chicken.

Bacteria on hand after handling raw meat.

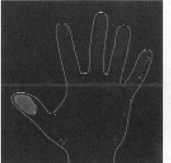

Notice how people often miss thumbs when washing.

See how thorough washing of hands removes bacteria.

Figure 6.6 Gruesome hands
© Food and Drink Federation (food**link** – www.food**link**.org.uk). Reproduced with permission.

Cuts and spots

We have already mentioned that healthy people can be carriers of *Staphylococcus aureus*. It is also found in many spots, boils and other skin conditions. It is essential that these affected areas are protected with waterproof dressings and gloves worn if necessary, to protect food from risk of contamination. All food handlers should report infected skin to their employer before they start work.

Clothes

All food handlers should wear clean washable protective clothing. What you will wear will depend on the extent to which you are involved in preparing and serving food.

- Hats: food handlers who prepare or serve food often wear hats or hairnets to prevent hair from falling into food. You are unlikely to prepare main meals. However, you will often be required to prepare snacks and serve snacks and meals. As a minimum, long hair should be tied or clipped back to prevent food being contaminated.
- Outdoor clothes: these should never be stored in the food area as they could contaminate food or surfaces. Your employer should provide separate lockers or hanging space.

- Jewellery: this should not be worn by food handlers. You employer may make exceptions for plain wedding rings and sleeper type earrings. Jewellery can harbour bacteria and it has been known for lost gemstones to contaminate food.

- Make up, cosmetics: the wearing of make up and strong smelling cosmetics should be avoided as this may contaminate/taint food. Nails should be kept short and unpainted as varnish may chip and contaminate food.

Reporting illness

If you are suffering from the symptoms of food-borne disease you must report this to your manager. These symptoms include:

- Diarrhoea
- Vomiting
- Nausea
- Ear, eye and nose discharges
- Septic wounds or any other skin condition.

The reasons for reporting these symptoms include:

- Prevention of food contamination.
- The legal requirement to report certain illnesses to the health authorities.
- The fact that you may need medical attention.
- You may need doctor's approval before you can continue to handle food.

Premises and equipment

These may vary, depending on whether or not you prepare snacks and meals from raw ingredients or reheat ready prepared meals. The design and construction of premises and equipment used are an important aspect of food hygiene. Although you may not have direct responsibility for this, you will need to be aware of the general principles involved so that you understand the part that you play in the workflow.

Suitability

All food preparation areas should be suitable for their intended purpose. Food preparation areas vary. However, there are some general principles of design which are important.

- Risk of food contamination minimised
- Facilities for temperature control
- Clean water supply
- Facilities for personal hygiene and first aid
- Suitable storage facilities for food and other non-food items
- Capable of being effectively cleaned
- Suitable drainage and other services
- Pest prevention
- Safe workflow and effective separation of clean and dirty activities

Figure 6.7 Nursery kitchen at Charlton House Nursery

Workflow

This is the route through the premises taken by the food from delivery through all the various stages of preparation to dispatch or consumption. Workflows that proceed in a straight line are best as this minimises the risk of contamination between raw and cooked food. Food handlers are also important in safe workflows and tasks should be planned to minimise movement around the kitchen.

Construction

The kitchen should be constructed of smooth and impervious materials which can be easily cleaned and disinfected. In addition, materials used should be resistant to cracking or chipping, non-toxic and resistant to rust. Using colour coded equipment is sometimes useful to remind staff about separating raw and cooked food.

Equipment

Equipment must be suitable for use in the kitchen and designed so that it can be easily cleaned. It is essential that there is adequate refrigerator space to store raw and cooked foods separately. The use of separate refrigerators for raw and cooked food is the best option.

Services and facilities

Good lighting and ventilation are important as well as facilities for washing food, equipment and maintaining personal hygiene. Wash hand basins must be separate from sinks used to wash food and food equipment. Wash hand basins must be provided with:

- Hot and cold running water preferably dispensed from foot or wrist operated taps
- Soap
- Drying materials such as paper towels

Cleaning and disinfection

Many childcare settings have dedicated cleaning staff; however, it is essential that if you are responsible for preparing snacks or meals that you 'clean as you go'. This section explains some of the principles associated with cleaning and suggests suitable methods for cleaning food contact surfaces and equipment.

Figure 6.8 Clean as you go

Purpose of cleaning

The aim of cleaning is to remove dirt. It involves energy, the effort of a machine or person and usually a combination of water and chemicals.

The benefits of effective cleaning include:

- Protecting food from contamination
- Avoiding attraction of pests
- Maintaining a safe environment, for example keeping floors free from slippery grease
- Creating a good impression for parents
- Complying with food hygiene legislation

Detergents are chemicals that you use to dissolve grease and remove dirt. An example would include washing up liquid.

Disinfection – is used to reduce bacteria to safe levels. It can be achieved by:

- Hot water at 82°C or above
- Steam
- Chemical disinfectants

Sanitisers are commonly used in the nurseries. These combine a detergent and disinfectant. They are particularly effective on surfaces that are relatively free of soil and grease such as work surfaces and sinks.

Sterilisation is the complete destruction of all micro-organisms. It is commonly used in nurseries to sterilise young babies' bottles and feeding equipment. It is mostly achieved by using an electric steriliser. Chemical methods are less frequently used.

What to clean and disinfect

All areas of the kitchen should be kept in a clean condition. Some equipment and areas may be cleaned less frequently, for example, once a day or at longer intervals. Equipment and areas that come into contact with food must be cleaned and disinfected frequently throughout the working period. This is referred to as 'clean as you go'.

Surfaces that come into contact with raw or high-risk foods, or anything which comes into contact with hands or other sources of contamination must be cleaned and disinfected/sanitised after every use. These include:

- Food contact surfaces such as chopping boards, work tops, knives, tongs and other utensils
- Hand contact surfaces such as handles, light switches, taps, and so on
- Major sources of contamination such as mop heads, cleaning equipment and waste bins

Examples of cleaning methods suitable for childcare settings

Cleaning a work surface

- Remove loose dirt.
- Wash surface with hot water and detergent.
- Rinse with hot water and clean cloth.
- Disinfect using a chemical disinfectant; follow the manufacturer's instructions and allow sufficient contact time.
- Rinse with clean water.
- Air dry or use a disposable paper towel.

Washing up

Most washing up will be done by a dishwasher. This is an effective way of cleaning and disinfecting food preparation items.

Washing by hand

You may still do this for small items and should always employ the two sink method.

- Remove particles of food.
- Wash items in the first sink which has hot water at 55°C and detergent. Replace the water if it becomes cool or dirty.
- Rinse in the second sink containing water at 82°C. Leave the items to soak for at least 30 seconds.
- Remove and leave to air dry.

Sterilising bottles

Before sterilising it is important to make sure that all items are washed thoroughly as milk residues can protect bacteria from the effects of heat or chemicals.

- Wash bottles and caps in hot soapy water, using a brush to reach all the inner parts of the bottle and turn the teat inside out and make sure that it is not blocked.
- Rinse everything under the tap before sterilising.

There are several ways to sterilise bottles:

- Boiling: place the bottles, teats and caps in a large pan of water; ensure that there are no air gaps in the bottles or teats and boil for at least five minutes.
- Cold water sterilisers: these consist of a large container filled with cold water and sterilising tablets. The bottles should be immersed for at least 30 minutes and any excess solution shaken off before use. The sterilising solution should be renewed at least every 24 hours.
- Steam sterilisers: the clean bottles are placed in the free standing unit and steamed for eight to ten minutes.
- Microwave sterilisers: these also use steam but are placed inside the microwave. Sterilisation usually takes place within about ten minutes.

Whichever method is used it is important not to contaminate the inside of bottles and teats by handling and manufacturers' instructions should always be followed.

Cleaning equipment

Cleaning equipment has the potential to be a major source of contamination. Cleaning cloths and tea towels are particularly problematic if they are used more than once. For this reason single use cloths are preferred particularly when disinfecting or sanitising. Childcare settings should have separate cleaning equipment, brushes, mops, and so on, for kitchens and on no account should these be used for cleaning bathrooms or other areas.

Food pests

All food premises have the potential to be contaminated by pests. Most nurseries will have engaged pest control companies who will visit the premises and surroundings on a frequent basis to check that there is no infestation.

Typical pests

These are anything living on human food and include:

- Insects such as flies, moths, ants, cockroaches and wasps
- Stored product pests such as beetles, mites, weevils and psocids
- Rodents such as rats and mice
- Birds, for example, pigeons

It is also important that pets are kept out of food areas and that feed bowls, cages and tanks are not cleaned in kitchens where food is being prepared.

Hazards associated with pests

Pests pose a variety of biological and physical hazards.

Biological hazards: pests commonly live in unhealthy places and pick up pathogenic bacteria. For example, flies live on animal droppings and rats live in sewers. This can easily be transferred to food.

Physical hazards can be caused by hair, fur, eggs, droppings and their own dead bodies.

Dealing with an infestation

If you suspect that you have an infestation, this should be reported to your manager who will contact a pest control company. If the infestation is serious then the local environmental health department should be contacted for specialist help and advice. In serious cases the childcare setting may have to close until the infestation is dealt with.

Preparing and serving food

Everyone wants to ensure that the children in their care receive safe and nutritious food. Carers have a legal responsibility to show that they have exercised utmost care and due diligence in their food preparation. This extends to using reputable suppliers who are complying with the appropriate food safety laws.

Opening checks at the start of each day

There are a number of checks that should take place at the beginning of each nursery day. These include making sure that:

- All equipment including fridge, freezer and cooker are working properly
- Staff are fit for work and wearing the appropriate protective clothing
- Food preparation areas and equipment are clean
- Plenty of hand washing and cleaning materials are available

Closing checks at the end of each day

These should take place at the end of the nursery day. These include making sure that:

- No food is left out
- Food past its use-by date is thrown away
- Dirty cleaning equipment has been cleaned or replaced
- Rubbish has been disposed of

The Food Standards Agency has recently piloted the Safer Food Better Business Food Safety Management System. This focuses on four main aspects of food safety management.

- Cooking
- Cleaning
- Chilling
- Cross-contamination

It is designed to help small food businesses comply with food hygiene regulations and encourages them to consider each of these issues in each stage of food preparation considered below.

Delivery

Even before supplies arrive at the childcare setting, fresh food will have started to deteriorate. It is particularly important that food is brought from a reputable supplier. Food that is obviously spoilt or at the wrong temperature on delivery should be rejected.

Date marks

Even if you check the appearance of food regularly, it is not always possible to detect contaminated food. For example, food contaminated by pathogenic bacteria may appear normal. Two different date codes are used in the UK to help food handlers to decide whether or not to use food.

Highly perishable foods such as meat, fish and ready to eat foods must be marked by a use by date. It is illegal to use or sell food that has gone past that date as it is likely to be unfit and could cause illness. Best before dates are used on less perishable items such as frozen food, dried fruit, cereals and canned food. This gives an indication to the consumer when the food is at its best quality. It is not good practice, but it is still legal to sell food marked with a best before date when it has gone past the date indicated.

Storage

Adequate facilities must be provided for the storage of perishable and non-perishable food items:

- Dry food stores must be kept cool, dry and ventilated.
- Refrigerators should be capable of maintaining food at storage temperatures of less than 5°C and provide for the adequate separation of raw and cooked foods. Most kitchens will have two fridges one for cooked and one for raw foods.

● Freezers must be capable of maintaining storage temperatures of less than −18°C.

Regardless of storage method used, stock rotation is essential. This involves using products with the shortest shelf life first. 'First in first out' and finally 'if in doubt chuck it out'.

Preparing food

Many of you will be involved in the preparation and serving of meals and snacks. This covers a range of activities and your involvement will depend of the nature of your job. The principles however remain the same.

Principles of food preparation

● Maintain good standards of personal hygiene.
● Protect food by preventing contamination, preventing multiplication of pathogens and/or destroying pathogenic micro-organisms.
● Make sure that all food contact surfaces are adequately cleaned and disinfected.
● Make sure that all open food is covered.
● Handle food as little as possible.
● Plan ahead and allow sufficient time for thawing, cooking and cooling. Plan to serve food as soon as possible after it is prepared.
● Keep food in storage until needed.
● Prepare the correct quantity of food and don't use leftovers.
● Don't leave high risk foods in the temperature danger zone for any longer than is necessary.
● Keep hot foods above 63°C.
● Keep cold foods below 5°C.
● Wash fruit, salads and vegetables before use.
● Use a clean spoon every time you taste the food.

Thawing frozen food

Some foods may be safely cooked from frozen and manufacturers' instructions should always be followed. Most frozen meat should be completely thawed before cooking so that adequate internal temperatures are reached during the cooking process. Thawing should take place in a specially designed cabinet or separate refrigerator. If a dual purpose refrigerator is used, extreme care must be taken to ensure that juices do not drip and contaminate other food.

Cooking

Cooking is a good way of destroying pathogenic micro-organisms. It is important that the food is heated to the correct temperature 75°C for at least two minutes. This can be checked by probing the core of the food towards the end of the cooking period.

Cooling hot food

Inadequate cooling can also lead to food-borne illness. When food is cooked too slowly, pathegenic bacteria are able to survive and multiply in the temperature danger zone. Whichever cooling methods are used, it is important to ensure that the temperature passes through the temperature danger zone quickly and that food is cooled to less than 5°C in less than 90 minutes.

It is important that hot food is never placed in refrigerators as this can raise the temperature and affect the safety of other foods stored there.

Reheating food

This may also cause food-borne illness and is best avoided. Problems can occur if reheating does not reach a high enough temperature and is a particular problem where preparation, cooking and subsequent storage is not hygienic. If you do have to reheat food:

- Never reheat the same item more than once.
- Always follow instructions on the food.
- Heat to at least 75°C for at least two minutes.
- Check core temperatures with a probe thermometer.

Hot and cold holding

This should be avoided. However, if you do need to prepare in advance and hold prior to serving, observe the following:

- Hot food must be stored above 63°C.
- Cold food stored at less than 5°C.

Getting trained

Food hygiene regulations state that all food handlers should be trained commensurate with their work activity. It is up to your supervisors to decide what is appropriate for you. As a minimum you should receive basic food hygiene training before you handle any food. You may also be offered the opportunity to take a food hygiene course. These qualifications are offered by various awarding bodies. For example the Chartered Institute of Environmental Health (CIEH) offers a range of recognised qualifications at various levels. The Foundation Certificate in Food Hygiene is a good entry level qualification for those responsible for preparing and serving food. For those in supervisory and management positions CIEH offer a range of appropriate qualifications including the intermediate and advanced certificates in food safety.

- All food handlers have a legal responsibility to keep food safe and comply with relevant food hygiene regulations.

- Food hazards may be chemical, biological or physical. Food poisoning and food-borne disease is mostly caused by pathogenic bacteria.

- Food poisoning is commonly caused by eating high-risk foods. They are described as high risk as they provide ideal conditions for bacteria to multiply to levels which may cause illness.

- Bacteria multiply every 10–20 minutes given ideal conditions including enough food, warmth, moisture and time. This process is known as binary fission.

- In order to keep food safe, it should always be stored outside the temperature danger zone of 5°C and 63°C. Cold food should be kept below 5°C and hot food above 63°C.

- Most bacteria are killed by cooking. Internal temperatures should reach at least 75°C.

- Good standards of personal hygiene are essential to food hygiene as human beings can be a source of food poisoning bacteria and foreign body contamination. Hand washing is an important aspect of this. Hands should be washed frequently and always after visiting the toilet, before food preparation, and after handling raw food or rubbish.

- All food premises should be constructed according to food hygiene regulations. Particular care should be taken to ensure that workflows are linear and that structural components and items of equipment can be effectively cleaned.

- All food preparation areas must be kept in a clean and hygienic condition. This is best achieved by designing a cleaning schedule, which specifies what is to be cleaned, by who, the method to be used and the frequency of cleaning.

- All food premises have the potential to be contaminated by pests. All suspected infestations should be reported to managers and dealt with by specialist pest control companies. If the infestation is serious then you should contact your local Environmental Health Department for advice.

- All childcare settings preparing and serving food should adopt a Food Safety Management System based on the principles of HACCP. Safer Food Better Business advocated by the Food Standards Agency is an example of such a system which is designed to help small food businesses comply with food hygiene regulations.

Find out more

- Check out the Health Protection Agency website http://www.hpa.org.uk for more information on food poisoning figures.

  For general information on food hygiene, CIEH publish several books which accompany their Foundation, Intermediate and Advanced certificates in Food Safety. Food Safety First Principles, Food Safety for Supervisors and Managing Food Safety.

- Check out the Food Standards Agency (FSA) website http://www.foodstandards.gov.uk for information on your legal responsibilities in relation to food safety and hygiene.

- Check out the following bad bug book on the following website http://www.cfsan.fda.gov/~mow/intro.html. If you want to look at some bacteria look at live cells at http://www.cellsalive.com/

- For further information on food allergy and intolerance see http://www.eatwell.gov.uk/healthissues/foodintolerance/

- More information about personal hygiene can be obtained from the Food Link website. http://www.foodlink.org.uk/factfile_c.asp?file=2&chapter=2

- Guidance for managers of childcare settings can be found in the following publication produced by the Health Protection Agency (HPA). Preventing person-to-person spread following gastro-intestinal infections, consult guidelines for public health physicians and environmental health officers at http://www.hpa.org.uk/cdph/issues/CDPHvol7/No4/guidelines2_4_04.pdf

- More information about kitchen hygiene can be obtained from the Food Link website: http://www.foodlink.org.uk/factfile_c.asp?file=2&chapter=1

- The following publications have excellent chapters on the science and management of effective cleaning: *Hygiene for Management* by Richard Sprenger Highfield Publications 2005 and *Managing Food Safety*, published by Chartered Institute of Environmental Health.

- FSA have developed a Safer Food Better Business Pack to help small food premises such as restaurants, cafés, take-aways and childcare providers comply with new regulations that apply from 1 January 2006: http://www.food.gov.uk/foodindustry/hygiene/sfbb/

- Many organisations offer food hygiene training and qualifications. One of the largest providers is the Chartered Institute of Environmental Health. They will be able to let you know about the types of qualifications that can be obtained and trainers and courses in your local area. Check their website for details: http://www.cieh.org/training/index.asp

Glossary

Amino acids The products of protein digestion. There are about 20 different types of amino acids needed by children. Some can be made in the body and some – the essential amino acids – cannot. They must be present in sufficient quantities in the diet. The nine essential amino acids required by children are: leucine, isoleucine, valine, threonine, methionine, phenylalanine, tryptophan, lysine and histidine.

Atheroma Fatty deposits on arteries. These can build up and harden on the walls of an artery – a condition known as atherosclerosis.

Bacteria Single celled micro-organisms that multiply by dividing into two. Some can cause illness or spoilage.

Binary fission The method of reproduction used by the bacteria by the division of the nucleus into two daughter nuclei, followed by a similar division of the cell body.

Cell The cell is the basic unit of all living organisms. Humans contain trillions of cells which require nourishment, produce energy, multiply and grow, and eventually die.

Cholesterol Cholesterol is a fat-like substance that is produced by the liver and is naturally present in many animal foods. Cholesterol is an essential component of cell membranes, the nervous system and some hormones. Too much cholesterol can cause the build up of atheroma.

Cleaning The process of removing soil, food residues, dirt, grease and other objectionable matter.

Co-factor Some enzymes need chemical or co-factor in order to function properly. Many of the vitamins and minerals act as co-factors.

Contamination The occurrence of any objectionable matter in the food or food environment.

Cross-contamination	The transfer of bacteria from contaminated foods (usually raw) to ready-to-eat foods by direct contact, drip or indirect contact using a vehicle such as hands or a cloth.
Detergent	A chemical or mixture of chemicals made of soap or synthetic substitutes; it facilitates the removal of grease and food particles from dishes and utensils and promotes cleanliness, so that all surfaces are readily accessible to the action of disinfectants.
Disinfectant	A chemical used for disinfection.
Disinfection	The reduction of micro-organisms to a level that will not lead to harmful contamination or spoilage of food.
Due diligence	The legal defence in the Food Safety Act 1990, that a person charged with an offence had taken all reasonable precautions and exercised all due diligence to avoid the committing of the offence by himself or herself or a person under his or her control.
Enzymes	Enzymes are proteins that control all the activities within a cell.
Fatty acids	The products of fat digestion. There are many different types of fatty acids and most can be made in the body. Essential fatty acids cannot be made in sufficient quantities and must be present in the diet – oily fish and some plant oils are particularly good sources.
Food-borne disease	Illness resulting from the consumption of food contaminated by pathogenic micro-organisms and/or their toxins. Characterised by having a low infective dose and no requirement for the multiplication of the organism within the food to cause illness.
Food poisoning	An acute illness of sudden onset caused by the recent consumption of contaminated or poisonous food.
Food handler	Any person in a food business who handles food, whether open or packaged (food includes ice and drink).
Food hygiene	All measures necessary to ensure the safety and wholesomeness of food during preparation, processing, manufacturing, storage, transport, distribution, handling and offering for sale or supply to the consumer, namely at all stages of the food chain.
Glycemic index (GI)	GI is a measure of the rate at which a carbohydrate-rich food will raise the blood glucose levels. Foods that raise blood glucose level quickly have a higher GI rating than foods that raise blood glucose level more slowly.
Hazard	The potential to cause harm to the consumer and can be microbiological, chemical or physical.

Hazard analysis critical control point (HACCP)	Any system which enables a food business to identify hazards, the points at which they occur and the introduction of measures to control them.
High risk foods	Ready-to-eat foods, which, under favourable conditions support the multiplication of pathogenic bacteria and are intended for consumption without treatment, which would destroy such organisms.
Hormones	Hormones control enzymes and chemical activities in our body. Insulin is an example of a hormone. It is produced in the pancreas and controls blood sugar levels throughout the body.
Metabolism	Metabolism is the sum of the chemical reactions that take place (in a child's body) – the breakdown of nutrients to produce energy and the production of new materials (biosynthesis).
Mycotoxins	Poisonous chemicals (toxins) produced by some moulds, for example, *Aspergillus flavus*.
Nutrients	Nutrients are substances that when consumed, digested and absorbed can be used to produce energy, growth and repair, or control these activities. The nutrients are: carbohydrates, proteins, fat (macronutrients), vitamins and minerals (micronutrients).
Pathogenic bacteria	Disease-producing bacteria.
Pest	Any living creature capable of directly or indirectly contaminating food.
Personal hygiene	Measures taken by food handlers to protect food from contamination from themselves.
Sanitiser	A chemical agent used for cleansing and disinfecting surfaces and equipment.
Satiated	A state when the appetite is fully satisfied.
Socio-economic classification	National Statistics Socio-Economic Classification (NS-SEC) is an occupationally based classification. There are eight classifications ranging from Class 1, higher managerial and professional occupations, to Class 8, never worked and long term unemployed.
Spores	A resistant resting-phase of bacteria, which protects them against adverse conditions.
Sterilisation	A process that destroys all living organisms.
Use-by date	The date mark required on high-risk, perishable pre-packed food, which must be stored under refrigeration. The food should be consumed on or before the use-by date. It is an offence to sell the food after its use-by date.
Viruses	Microscopic pathogens that multiply in the living cells of their hosts.

References and bibliography

Barasi, M.E. (2003) *Human Nutrition: A Health perspective.* London: Hodder Arnold.

Brazelton, T.B. and Sparrow, J.D. (2004) *Feeding Your Child The Brazelton Way.* Cambridge, MA: Da Capo Press.

Caroline Walker Trust (1998) *Eating Well for Under-5's in Child Care. Practical and Nutritional Guidelines. Report of a Expert Working Group.* London: The Caroline Walker Trust.

Crawley, H. (2005) *Nutrient-Based Standards for School Food. A Summary of the Standards and Recommendations of the Caroline Walker Trust and the National Heart Forum.*

Davies, S. (2005) *Which Policy Report. Which Choice?* London: Consumers Association.

Department for Education and Skills (DfES 314/2000) (2005) *Healthy School Lunches for Pupils in Nursery Schools/Units. Guidance for School Caterers on Implementing National Nutritional Standards.* London: The Stationery Office.

Department of Health (2005) *Choosing a Better Diet: A Food and Health Action Plan.* London: The Stationery Office.

Engel, DMD., MacDonald, D., Nash, C. (2001) *Managing Food Safety.* London: Chadwick House Limited.

Food and Drink Federation (Food Link) Website. www.foodlink.org.uk (accessed 3/1/2006).

Food Standards Agency Website www.foodstandards.gov.uk (accessed 3/1/2006).

Hedesy, J.H. and Budd, K.S. (1998) *Childhood Feeding Disorders: Biobehavioural Assessment and Intervention.* Baltimore, MD: Brookes Publishing Co.

Herbert, M. (1996) *Coping with Children's Feeding Problems and Bedtime Battles. Parent, Adolescent and Child Training Skills.* London: The British Psychological Society.

House of Commons Health Committee (2004) *Obesity Third report of session 2003–4.* London: The Stationery Office.

Karmel, A. (1999) *Feeding your Baby and Toddler.* The Complete Cook Book. London: Dorling Kindersley Limited.

Lean, M.E.J. (2006) *Fox and Cameron's Food Science, Nutrition and Health,* seventh edn. London: Hodder Arnold.

MAFF (1995) *Manual of Nutrition.* London: The Stationery Office.

Morgan J.B. and Dickerson J.W.T (2002) *Nutrition in Early Life.* Chichester: John Wiley and Sons.

Nash, C. (2006) *Food Safety First Principles*. London: Chadwick House Group Limited.

Office for Standards in Education (HMI2292) (2004) *Starting Early: Food and Nutrition Education of Young Children*. London: The Stationery Office.

Parliamentary Office of Science and Technology (2003a) *POST Report 199 Improving Children's Diet*. London: Parliamentary Bookshop.

Parliamentary Office of Science and Technology (2003b) *POST Report 203 Childhood Obesity*. London: Parliamentary Bookshop.

Roberts, S.B., Heyman, M.B. and Tracy, L. (1999) *Feeding Your Child for Lifelong Health*. New York: Bantam Books.

Sprenger, R. (2005) *Hygiene for Management*. London: Highfield Publications.

Stevenson, S., Nash, C. (2000) *Food Safety for Supervisors*. London: Chadwick House Group Limited.

Taylor, J. (1998) *Early Childhood Studies: An holistic Introduction*. London: Hodder Arnold.

Wall, P.G. (1996) 'Food poisoning: notifications, laboratory reports and outbreaks – where do the statistics come from and what do they mean'. Communicable Disease Review, 6: 93–100.

Wardlaw, G.M. (2003) *Contemporary Nutrition: Issues and Insights*, fifth edn. Maidenhead: McGraw Hill.

Worthington Roberts, B.S. and Rodwell Williams, S. (eds) (2000) *Nutrition throughout the Life Cycle*. Maidenhead: McGraw Hill.

Index